a-6900

W9-ATL-851

NELSON
AND
WINNIE
MANDELA

NELSON
AND
WINNIE
MANDELA

John Vail

CHELSEA HOUSE PUBLISHERS
NEW YORK
PHILADELPHIA

Chelsea House Publishers
EDITOR-IN-CHIEF: Nancy Toff
EXECUTIVE EDITOR: Remmel T. Nunn
MANAGING EDITOR: Karyn Gullen Browne
COPY CHIEF: Juliann Barbato
PICTURE EDITOR: Adrian G. Allen
ART DIRECTOR: Maria Epes
MANUFACTURING MANAGER: Gerald Levine

World Leaders—Past & Present
SENIOR EDITOR: John W. Selfridge

Staff for NELSON AND WINNIE MANDELA:
COPY EDITOR: Karen Hammonds
DEPUTY COPY CHIEF: Ellen Scordato
EDITORIAL ASSISTANT: Heather Lewis
PICTURE RESEARCHER: Linda Peer
ASSISTANT ART DIRECTOR: Laurie Jewell
DESIGNER: David Murray
PRODUCTION COORDINATOR: Joseph Romano
COVER ILLUSTRATION: Bill Tinker

Copyright © 1989 Chelsea House Publishers, a division of
Main Line Book Co. All rights reserved. Printed and bound in
the United States of America.

3 5 7 9 8 6 4 2

Library of Congress Cataloging in Publication Data

Vail, John J.
Nelson and Winnie Mandela.

(World leaders past & present)
Bibliography: p.
Includes index.
   Summary: Records the couple's struggles against South Africa's
racial policies, which led to Nelson's imprisonment and Winnie's
banishment to a remote part of the Orange Free State.

1. Mandela, Nelson, 1918–   .—Juvenile literature.
2. Mandela, Winnie—Juvenile literature. 3. Banned persons
(South Africa)—Biography—Juvenile literature. 4. Civil
rights workers—South Africa—Biography—Juvenile
literature. 5. Anti-apartheid movements—South Africa—
Juvenile literature. [1. Mandela, Nelson, 1918–
2. Mandela, Winnie. 3. Civil rights workers—South Africa.
4. South Africa—Race relations. 5. Blacks—Biography]
I. Title. II. Series.
DT779.95.M36V35   1988   323.4'092'2   87-32556

ISBN 1-55546-841-1
    0-7910-0586-0 (pbk.)

Contents

JOHN ADAMS
JOHN QUINCY ADAMS
KONRAD ADENAUER
ALEXANDER THE GREAT
SALVADOR ALLENDE
MARC ANTONY
CORAZON AQUINO
YASIR ARAFAT
KING ARTHUR
HAFEZ al-ASSAD
KEMAL ATATÜRK
ATTILA
CLEMENT ATTLEE
AUGUSTUS CAESAR
MENACHEM BEGIN
DAVID BEN-GURION
OTTO VON BISMARCK
LÉON BLUM
SIMON BOLÍVAR
CESARE BORGIA
WILLY BRANDT
LEONID BREZHNEV
JULIUS CAESAR
JOHN CALVIN
JIMMY CARTER
FIDEL CASTRO
CATHERINE THE GREAT
CHARLEMAGNE
CHIANG KAI-SHEK
WINSTON CHURCHILL
GEORGES CLEMENCEAU
CLEOPATRA
CONSTANTINE THE GREAT
HERNÁN CORTÉS
OLIVER CROMWELL
GEORGES-JACQUES
   DANTON
JEFFERSON DAVIS
MOSHE DAYAN
CHARLES DE GAULLE
EAMON DE VALERA
EUGENE DEBS
DENG XIAOPING
BENJAMIN DISRAELI
ALEXANDER DUBČEK
FRANÇOIS & JEAN-CLAUDE
   DUVALIER
DWIGHT EISENHOWER
ELEANOR OF AQUITAINE
ELIZABETH I
FAISAL
FERDINAND & ISABELLA
FRANCISCO FRANCO
BENJAMIN FRANKLIN

FREDERICK THE GREAT
INDIRA GANDHI
MOHANDAS GANDHI
GIUSEPPE GARIBALDI
AMIN & BASHIR GEMAYEL
GENGHIS KHAN
WILLIAM GLADSTONE
MIKHAIL GORBACHEV
ULYSSES S. GRANT
ERNESTO "CHE" GUEVARA
TENZIN GYATSO
ALEXANDER HAMILTON
DAG HAMMARSKJÖLD
HENRY VIII
HENRY OF NAVARRE
PAUL VON HINDENBURG
HIROHITO
ADOLF HITLER
HO CHI MINH
KING HUSSEIN
IVAN THE TERRIBLE
ANDREW JACKSON
JAMES I
WOJCIECH JARUZELSKI
THOMAS JEFFERSON
JOAN OF ARC
POPE JOHN XXIII
POPE JOHN PAUL II
LYNDON JOHNSON
BENITO JUÁREZ
JOHN KENNEDY
ROBERT KENNEDY
JOMO KENYATTA
AYATOLLAH KHOMEINI
NIKITA KHRUSHCHEV
KIM IL SUNG
MARTIN LUTHER KING, JR.
HENRY KISSINGER
KUBLAI KHAN
LAFAYETTE
ROBERT E. LEE
VLADIMIR LENIN
ABRAHAM LINCOLN
DAVID LLOYD GEORGE
LOUIS XIV
MARTIN LUTHER
JUDAS MACCABEUS
JAMES MADISON
NELSON & WINNIE
   MANDELA
MAO ZEDONG
FERDINAND MARCOS
GEORGE MARSHALL

MARY, QUEEN OF SCOTS
TOMÁS MASARYK
GOLDA MEIR
KLEMENS VON METTERNICH
JAMES MONROE
HOSNI MUBARAK
ROBERT MUGABE
BENITO MUSSOLINI
NAPOLÉON BONAPARTE
GAMAL ABDEL NASSER
JAWAHARLAL NEHRU
NERO
NICHOLAS II
RICHARD NIXON
KWAME NKRUMAH
DANIEL ORTEGA
MOHAMMED REZA PAHLAVI
THOMAS PAINE
CHARLES STEWART
   PARNELL
PERICLES
JUAN PERÓN
PETER THE GREAT
POL POT
MUAMMAR el-QADDAFI
RONALD REAGAN
CARDINAL RICHELIEU
MAXIMILIEN ROBESPIERRE
ELEANOR ROOSEVELT
FRANKLIN ROOSEVELT
THEODORE ROOSEVELT
ANWAR SADAT
HAILE SELASSIE
PRINCE SIHANOUK
JAN SMUTS
JOSEPH STALIN
SUKARNO
SUN YAT-SEN
TAMERLANE
MOTHER TERESA
MARGARET THATCHER
JOSIP BROZ TITO
TOUSSAINT L'OUVERTURE
LEON TROTSKY
PIERRE TRUDEAU
HARRY TRUMAN
QUEEN VICTORIA
LECH WALESA
GEORGE WASHINGTON
CHAIM WEIZMANN
WOODROW WILSON
XERXES
EMILIANO ZAPATA
ZHOU ENLAI

CHELSEA HOUSE PUBLISHERS

ON LEADERSHIP

Arthur M. Schlesinger, jr.

LEADERSHIP, it may be said, is really what makes the world go round. Love no doubt smooths the passage; but love is a private transaction between consenting adults. Leadership is a public transaction with history. The idea of leadership affirms the capacity of individuals to move, inspire, and mobilize masses of people so that they act together in pursuit of an end. Sometimes leadership serves good purposes, sometimes bad; but whether the end is benign or evil, great leaders are those men and women who leave their personal stamp on history.

Now, the very concept of leadership implies the proposition that individuals can make a difference. This proposition has never been universally accepted. From classical times to the present day, eminent thinkers have regarded individuals as no more than the agents and pawns of larger forces, whether the gods and goddesses of the ancient world or, in the modern era, race, class, nation, the dialectic, the will of the people, the spirit of the times, history itself. Against such forces, the individual dwindles into insignificance.

So contends the thesis of historical determinism. Tolstoy's great novel *War and Peace* offers a famous statement of the case. Why, Tolstoy asked, did millions of men in the Napoleonic Wars, denying their human feelings and their common sense, move back and forth across Europe slaughtering their fellows? "The war," Tolstoy answered, "was bound to happen simply because it was bound to happen." All prior history predetermined it. As for leaders, they, Tolstoy said, "are but the labels that serve to give a name to an end and, like labels, they have the least possible connection with the event." The greater the leader, "the more conspicuous the inevitability and the predestination of every act he commits." The leader, said Tolstoy, is "the slave of history."

Determinism takes many forms. Marxism is the determinism of class. Nazism the determinism of race. But the idea of men and women as the slaves of history runs athwart the deepest human instincts. Rigid determinism abolishes the idea of human freedom—

the assumption of free choice that underlies every move we make, every word we speak, every thought we think. It abolishes the idea of human responsibility, since it is manifestly unfair to reward or punish people for actions that are by definition beyond their control. No one can live consistently by any deterministic creed. The Marxist states prove this themselves by their extreme susceptibility to the cult of leadership.

More than that, history refutes the idea that individuals make no difference. In December 1931 a British politician crossing Park Avenue in New York City between 76th and 77th Streets around 10:30 P.M. looked in the wrong direction and was knocked down by an automobile—a moment, he later recalled, of a man aghast, a world aglare: "I do not understand why I was not broken like an eggshell or squashed like a gooseberry." Fourteen months later an American politician, sitting in an open car in Miami, Florida, was fired on by an assassin; the man beside him was hit. Those who believe that individuals make no difference to history might well ponder whether the next two decades would have been the same had Mario Constasino's car killed Winston Churchill in 1931 and Giuseppe Zangara's bullet killed Franklin Roosevelt in 1933. Suppose, in addition, that Adolf Hitler had been killed in the street fighting during the Munich *Putsch* of 1923 and that Lenin had died of typhus during World War I. What would the 20th century be like now?

For better or for worse, individuals do make a difference. "The notion that a people can run itself and its affairs anonymously," wrote the philosopher William James, "is now well known to be the silliest of absurdities. Mankind does nothing save through initiatives on the part of inventors, great or small, and imitation by the rest of us—these are the sole factors in human progress. Individuals of genius show the way, and set the patterns, which common people then adopt and follow."

Leadership, James suggests, means leadership in thought as well as in action. In the long run, leaders in thought may well make the greater difference to the world. But, as Woodrow Wilson once said, "Those only are leaders of men, in the general eye, who lead in action. . . . It is at their hands that new thought gets its translation into the crude language of deeds." Leaders in thought often invent in solitude and obscurity, leaving to later generations the tasks of imitation. Leaders in action—the leaders portrayed in this series—have to be effective in their own time.

And they cannot be effective by themselves. They must act in response to the rhythms of their age. Their genius must be adapted, in a phrase of William James's, "to the receptivities of the moment." Leaders are useless without followers. "There goes the mob," said the French politician hearing a clamor in the streets. "I am their leader. I must follow them." Great leaders turn the inchoate emotions of the mob to purposes of their own. They seize on the opportunities of their time, the hopes, fears, frustrations, crises, potentialities. They succeed when events have prepared the way for them, when the community is awaiting to be aroused, when they can provide the clarifying and organizing ideas. Leadership ignites the circuit between the individual and the mass and thereby alters history.

It may alter history for better or for worse. Leaders have been responsible for the most extravagant follies and most monstrous crimes that have beset suffering humanity. They have also been vital in such gains as humanity has made in individual freedom, religious and racial tolerance, social justice, and respect for human rights.

There is no sure way to tell in advance who is going to lead for good and who for evil. But a glance at the gallery of men and women in *World Leaders—Past and Present* suggests some useful tests.

One test is this: Do leaders lead by force or by persuasion? By command or by consent? Through most of history leadership was exercised by the divine right of authority. The duty of followers was to defer and to obey. "Theirs not to reason why / Theirs but to do and die." On occasion, as with the so-called enlightened despots of the 18th century in Europe, absolutist leadership was animated by humane purposes. More often, absolutism nourished the passion for domination, land, gold, and conquest and resulted in tyranny.

The great revolution of modern times has been the revolution of equality. The idea that all people should be equal in their legal condition has undermined the old structure of authority, hierarchy, and deference. The revolution of equality has had two contrary effects on the nature of leadership. For equality, as Alexis de Tocqueville pointed out in his great study *Democracy in America*, might mean equality in servitude as well as equality in freedom.

"I know of only two methods of establishing equality in the political world," Tocqueville wrote. "Rights must be given to every citizen, or none at all to anyone . . . save one, who is the master of all." There was no middle ground "between the sovereignty of all and the absolute power of one man." In his astonishing prediction of 20th-century totalitarian dictatorship, Tocqueville explained how the revolution of equality could lead to the *"Führerprinzip"* and more terrible absolutism than the world had ever known.

But when rights are given to every citizen and the sovereignty of all is established, the problem of leadership takes a new form, becomes more exacting than ever before. It is easy to issue commands and enforce them by the rope and the stake, the concentration camp and the *gulag.* It is much harder to use argument and achievement to overcome opposition and win consent. The Founding Fathers of the United States understood the difficulty. They believed that history had given them the opportunity to decide, as Alexander Hamilton wrote in the first Federalist Paper, whether men are indeed capable of basing government on "reflection and choice, or whether they are forever destined to depend . . . on accident and force."

Government by reflection and choice called for a new style of leadership and a new quality of followership. It required leaders to be responsive to popular concerns, and it required followers to be active and informed participants in the process. Democracy does not eliminate emotion from politics; sometimes it fosters demagoguery; but it is confident that, as the greatest of democratic leaders put it, you cannot fool all of the people all of the time. It measures leadership by results and retires those who overreach or falter or fail.

It is true that in the long run despots are measured by results too. But they can postpone the day of judgment, sometimes indefinitely, and in the meantime they can do infinite harm. It is also true that democracy is no guarantee of virtue and intelligence in government, for the voice of the people is not necessarily the voice of God. But democracy, by assuring the right of opposition, offers built-in resistance to the evils inherent in absolutism. As the theologian Reinhold Niebuhr summed it up, "Man's capacity for justice makes democracy possible, but man's inclination to injustice makes democracy necessary."

A second test for leadership is the end for which power is sought. When leaders have as their goal the supremacy of a master race or the promotion of totalitarian revolution or the acquisition and exploitation of colonies or the protection of greed and privilege or the preservation of personal power, it is likely that their leadership will do little to advance the cause of humanity. When their goal is the abolition of slavery, the liberation of women, the enlargement of opportunity for the poor and powerless, the extension of equal rights to racial minorities, the defense of the freedoms of expression and opposition, it is likely that their leadership will increase the sum of human liberty and welfare.

Leaders have done great harm to the world. They have also conferred great benefits. You will find both sorts in this series. Even "good" leaders must be regarded with a certain wariness. Leaders are not demigods; they put on their trousers one leg after another just like ordinary mortals. No leader is infallible, and every leader needs to be reminded of this at regular intervals. Irreverence irritates leaders but is their salvation. Unquestioning submission corrupts leaders and demeans followers. Making a cult of a leader is always a mistake. Fortunately hero worship generates its own antidote. "Every hero," said Emerson, "becomes a bore at last."

The signal benefit the great leaders confer is to embolden the rest of us to live according to our own best selves, to be active, insistent, and resolute in affirming our own sense of things. For great leaders attest to the reality of human freedom against the supposed inevitabilities of history. And they attest to the wisdom and power that may lie within the most unlikely of us, which is why Abraham Lincoln remains the supreme example of great leadership. A great leader, said Emerson, exhibits new possibilities to all humanity. "We feed on genius. . . . Great men exist that there may be greater men."

Great leaders, in short, justify themselves by emancipating and empowering their followers. So humanity struggles to master its destiny, remembering with Alexis de Tocqueville: "It is true that around every man a fatal circle is traced beyond which he cannot pass; but within the wide verge of that circle he is powerful and free; as it is with man, so with communities."

1

Birth of a Freedom Fighter

The atmosphere in the Pretoria courthouse was electric. The tall black man in the witness box had been accused of attempting to overthrow the South African government by sabotage and guerrilla warfare, and for the past five months the prosecution had presented an endless stream of documents and exhibits to prove his guilt. If convicted, the 45-year-old revolutionary could be sentenced to death. Now, on April 23, 1964, he was about to testify in his own behalf.

Nelson Mandela glanced at the spectator's gallery, where his young wife Winnie sat. Their eyes met, and she smiled encouragingly. He rose, and in a clear, compelling voice he began to read his statement. Mandela readily admitted that he had tried to bring down the white government, but he explained that his actions were "the result of a calm and sober assessment of the political situation that had arisen after many years of tyranny, exploitation and oppression of my people by the whites."

Any thinking African in this country is driven continuously to a conflict between his conscience and the law.
—NELSON MANDELA

For more than 40 years, Nelson Mandela has been a leader of the black nationalist movement in South Africa. Imprisoned since 1962 for his political beliefs, he has been a source of courage and inspiration to the country's oppressed black majority.

THIS PARK BELONGS TO THE CITIZENS AND IS UNDER THEIR PROTECTION. NO DOGS, PEDAL AND MOTOR CYCLES ARE ALLOWED IN THESE GROUNDS. NATIVES ARE NOT ALLOWED IN THESE GROUNDS, EXCEPT IN ATTENDANCE ON EUROPEANS OR IN CHARGE OF EUROPEAN CHILDREN. ANY PERSON WHO SHALL PICK, DAMAGE, REMOVE OR DESTROY ANY FLOWERS, PLANT, SHRUB OR TREE WILL BE PROSECUTED.

A sign on a fence printed in English and Afrikaans, the language of South Africans of Dutch descent, warns blacks (natives) not to trespass on park grounds unless accompanied by a white. In the early 1960s, Mandela waged a sabotage campaign against government property to protest its racist apartheid policies.

With these brave words, Nelson Mandela denounced apartheid, the doctrine of racial segregation and white supremacy espoused by the National party that has ruled South Africa since 1948. He also lamented the injustice and inequality of a system of government under which the white minority has subjugated the African majority. Fifty years of nonviolent protest by Africans (blacks) against white supremacy had failed to bring meaningful reform and instead had prompted more violence and repression by the government. Now, Mandela said, Africans had two choices in this racist society — to submit to oppression or to fight.

Mandela went on to explain that he had dedicated his entire life to the struggle for a democratic society in South Africa that would guarantee equality and racial harmony for all. "If needs be," he said, "it is an ideal for which I am prepared to die." A hush fell over the stunned courtroom, broken only by the sobs of spectators moved by Mandela's eloquence. These were Nelson Mandela's last public words in South Africa. Six weeks later, he and seven other defendants were found guilty and sentenced to life imprisonment.

Several thousand supporters gathered outside the courthouse to give the prisoners a spirited send-off. The huge crowd chanted freedom songs and held up banners proclaiming We Are Proud of Our Leaders and No Tears: Our Future is Bright. Winnie Mandela, with her two daughters at her side, waited for one last glimpse of her husband. As the armored vehicle holding the prisoners drove away, Mandela and his comrades defiantly thrust their fists through the barred windows and shouted "Amandla!" (power), the slogan of the outlawed African National Congress (ANC). The men were flown to Cape Town and then taken by ferryboat to Robben Island, a maximum-security facility for South Africa's political prisoners. Today, nearly 25 years later, Nelson Mandela is still imprisoned in South Africa. An international symbol of courage, he is the most famous prisoner in the world.

Winnie Mandela (right) holds one of her daughters as she waits for her husband to emerge from the courthouse after he was sentenced to life in prison. Convicted in 1964 of trying to overthrow the government, Nelson Mandela has been allowed no direct contact with the public.

Nelson Mandela's decision to become a committed revolutionary can be understood only in light of the unique historical evolution of South African society. The current white leaders of South Africa are descendants of Dutch settlers who landed at the tip of the African continent in 1652 and established Cape Town, the first white settlement in South Africa. The whites, known as Afrikaners, insist that their Dutch ancestors arrived at the cape at the same time that the ancestors of modern Africans were migrating southward into the area, and thus they claim that they have as much right to South Africa as the Africans. However, all historical evidence demonstrates that black farmers from central Africa had moved to South Africa innumerable generations before the whites' arrival.

A long and violent struggle for control of the land took place between the white invaders and the African tribes. In the Cape Province, where the African tribe known as the Khoi Khoi had neither enough people nor sufficient military expertise to prevent large-scale European settlement, the Afrikaners seized the land and cattle of the Khoi Khoi for their own use and forced the defeated Africans to become exploited workers in the white economy. It was a pattern that would be repeated time and again over the next 200 years.

A group of Afrikaners rest after a successful day of hunting bushbucks in 1888. The descendants of Dutch immigrants who first settled in South Africa in 1652, the Afrikaners long have managed to divide and dominate the country's native black population.

From 1770 to 1880, the Afrikaners fought a series of bloody wars with African tribes such as the Xhosa, Zulu, Sotho, Venda, and Thembu as they expanded into the territory beyond the Cape Province. These battles inspired future generations' tales of the heroic African resistance, but by pitting chieftain against rival African chieftain and subduing all rebellion with their superior firepower, the Afrikaners won control of the country. Unlike the North and South American Indians, whose population was drastically reduced by disease as a result of contact with whites, the Africans overwhelmingly outnumbered the whites in South Africa and kept possession of most of the actual territory.

Then, in 1806, Great Britain captured the Cape Colony from the Dutch. During the next 25 years, the British enacted a series of reforms, abolishing slavery, easing the Afrikaners' system of forced labor, and establishing a constitution that granted the Africans legal equality with the whites. The Afrikaners so resented this interference and so furiously objected to any equality between whites and blacks that they abandoned the Cape Colony and fled British control.

Zulu chiefs and warriors pose in war dress in front of a grass hut, or *kraal*. One of the Afrikaners' chief national holidays celebrates their victory over a Zulu army at Blood River in 1838, a battle that led to the downfall of the once mighty Zulu nation.

British troops prepare for battle in South Africa in 1899. The Afrikaners resented the less restrictive racial policies enforced by the British, who seized control of the area in 1806. Land disputes between the two groups erupted into the Boer War, which the British won after a fierce struggle.

In 1836, 8,000 Afrikaners set out in ox-drawn wagons on a "Great Trek" to the interior, where they established two independent Afrikaner republics — the Orange Free State and the Transvaal Republic. The niece of a leader of the trek explained that what drove them "to such lengths" was the Africans' "being placed on an equal footing with Christians, contrary to the laws of God and the natural distinctions of race and religion." The Afrikaners in the Cape Colony were determined to establish an even more rigorous system of racial domination than had ever existed.

The independent Afrikaner republics were recognized by the British colonial authorities that controlled southern Africa in the 1880s, but Great Britain still hoped one day to form a British-dominated federation of the republics and the Cape provinces. The discovery of gold in the Transvaal in 1886 provided the economic rationalization and political pretext that Britain needed to implement such a scheme. Great Britain feared that the Afrikaner republics could become wealthy and powerful challengers to British control. In 1899, tensions, pressures, and intrigues erupted into the Boer War, a three-year battle between the Afrikaners (often called Boers) in the two republics and Great Britain.

The greatly outnumbered Afrikaners fought a desperate guerrilla war, but Great Britain mounted a ferocious countercampaign, burning farms and crops and herding women and children into horrible concentration camps as hostages. Transvaal and the Orange Free State surrendered, joining Cape and Natal provinces to form a new dominion of the British Commonwealth of Nations, the Union of South Africa, which was formally established in 1910.

British colonial control in no way affected the Afrikaners' domination of the black majority. Control was maintained by limiting blacks' power and privileges through segregation, which was deliberate public policy in South Africa. The law specified that blacks and whites should have completely separate public facilities, political institutions, and living areas. Two laws in particular, the Natives Land Act

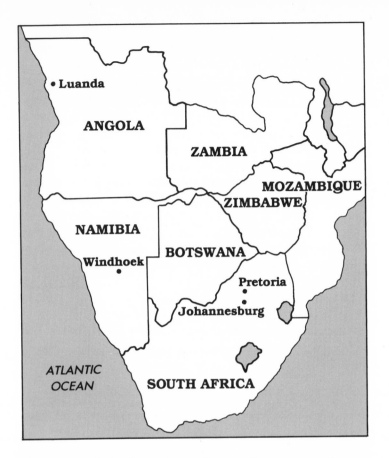

of 1913 and the "pass laws," served as cornerstones of white supremacy.

The Natives Land Act, which uprooted blacks from their farms and homes and restricted them to special "native reserves," created a grossly inequitable division of territory in the country. The minority whites were allocated 87 percent of the land; the majority blacks were given only 13 percent in the already crowded all-black reserves. The Land Act prohibited African land purchase outside the reserves, and by preventing large numbers of rural Africans from being self-sufficient farmers, it ensured that white farmers and industrialists would have an inexhaustible supply of cheap black labor.

Not all blacks were kept in the reserves, however. A substantial minority were allowed to live in the cities because they performed essential economic services for the whites. The flow of Africans was strictly regulated by an elaborate system of "influx

Police examine passbooks of black workers in Johannesburg. Enacted in the 1880s as a means of controlling the movements of the nonwhite population, the passbook laws required blacks to obtain permits to work and live outside of their home areas.

controls." Blacks were not allowed into the city unless they had permanent jobs; they often were forced to leave their families behind, and they could be returned to the reserves when their labor was no longer required. Most Africans lived in isolated townships (ghettos) and had to spend long hours traveling into the city for employment.

Pass laws also reinforced white supremacy by ensuring Afrikaner control over African movement. An African needed a pass to obtain a job, to travel, or to be out after curfew. Blacks had to carry their passbooks at all times; any white could ask to see a pass at any time, and failure to produce one usually led to imprisonment and loss of one's job. Normal political channels offered no hope of change because the black majority could elect only a handful of token, nonvoting white representatives to the white parliament. Mass protests were the Africans' only recourse.

Into this troubled land, Nelson Mandela was born on July 18, 1918, near Umtata, the capital town of the Transkei native reserve. Mandela's Xhosa name, Rolihlahla, which means "stirring up trouble," now seems almost a prediction of his future political activism, but in 1918 the baby's family background seemed to promise a life of respectability and status. His family was of royal tribal lineage; his father, Henry Gadla Mandela, was chief counsel to the paramount chief of the Thembu tribe. His mother, Nosekeni, a quiet and unassuming woman, was a great source of strength and inspiration for Nelson.

Nelson lived a typically carefree childhood, helping to plow the fields and tend the sheep and cattle on the rolling hills of the Transkei. At night he would sit by the fire and listen to exciting tales told by white-haired tribal elders. He learned of the days when Africans lived in peaceful, democratic communities, free to travel throughout their own country. He was particularly spellbound by the legends of the great warrior generals who had fought courageous and heroic battles against the white invaders. These stories inspired him to dream of following in his ancestors' footsteps in the struggle for African freedom.

When Nelson was 12 years old, his father became seriously ill and sent for the paramount chief to plan Nelson's future. He hoped his son would be raised in the chief's household after his death. As Nelson Mandela's biographer Mary Benson recounts, Henry Mandela proudly told the chief: "This is my only son. I can say from the way he speaks to his sisters and friends that his inclination is to help the nation." After his father died, Nelson lived for several years at the chief's grand palace, where his favorite activity was to observe the trials conducted by the paramount chief to settle disputes between tribal leaders. Nelson enjoyed the thrilling give-and-take of cross-examination, and he hoped someday to test his own skills as a lawyer.

Nelson attended a Methodist high school and then enrolled in Fort Hare College in the eastern cape city of Alice. Fort Hare College was a distinguished institution that had educated many black leaders and professionals in South Africa and other African nations. One of Nelson's fellow students and close friends was Oliver Tambo, who would become a lifelong associate. Besides having an excellent academic record, Nelson was an outstanding speaker and campus leader; he was elected to serve on the students' representative council, which regulated student activities and curriculum at the college. When the white authorities reduced the powers of the council, a handful of activists, including Nelson, launched a student boycott of the university to protest the action.

Nelson was suspended. He returned home, where he was ordered by the paramount chief to abandon the protest and resume his studies. To make matters worse, the chief had selected a bride for Nelson and had begun making secret preparations for the wedding. Nelson was horrified that his guardian had failed to consult him about such an important personal matter, and he suddenly realized that the chief was about to begin grooming him to become a future chieftain — a career of which he wanted no part. His only alternative, he decided, was to run away to Johannesburg and stake out a life of his own in the big city.

A mother and child stand near a barbed-wire fence that marks the border of a village in a homeland area. In 1913, the South African government passed the Natives Land Act, which appropriated 87 percent of the land for the white minority. Blacks were forced to live on crowded and often barren native reserves.

2

A New Generation Emerges

The 23-year-old Mandela was unprepared for the shock of Johannesburg, the bustling City of Gold. The tall, aristocratic-looking young man spent his first day wandering about, bedazzled by the nonstop traffic, the tall buildings, and the huge crowds. With only enough money to cover his living expenses for a few days, Mandela's first priority was to find a job. His best opportunity would be at one of the thriving gold mines, so he dressed in his finest suit and visited the mine's personnel office, seeking employment as a clerical worker. The personnel director, amused by Mandela's naïveté, informed him that the only available position was as a security guard, but promised that if he worked hard enough, he could look forward to being promoted to clerk one day.

African National Congress (ANC) activist Walter Sisulu encouraged Mandela to become strongly involved in the country's budding black nationalist movement. In the mid-1940s, they became two of the foremost leaders of the ANC's militant protest organization, the Youth League.

> *Groomed from childhood for respectability, status and sheltered living, he was now thrown into the melting-pot of urban survival.*
> —MARY BENSON
> author, on Mandela coming to Johannesburg

Mandela worked for a few days as a guard at a mining compound after he first arrived in Johannesburg. His first encounters with the wretched conditions of the black workers in the city convinced him that the best weapon against white domination was a strong black nationalist movement.

Tall, gangly, and somewhat comical-looking in his ill-fitting policeman's uniform, Mandela was assigned to the graveyard shift, from 10:00 P.M. to 6:00 A.M.. His job was to guard the entrance to the black miners' compound, for the workers were confined to their shabby quarters after dark to prevent their going into town. After a few days, however, Mandela learned that an emissary of the paramount chief had been asking questions about him at the mine office, and he promptly decided to end his brief career in law enforcement.

Mandela found an inexpensive apartment in the black township of Alexandra, on the outskirts of Johannesburg, and in time became a close friend of a genial man named Walter Sisulu. Mandela told Sisulu of his troubles with his tribal relatives and how he longed to return to his pre-law studies. Sisulu, who owned a small real-estate agency, loaned Mandela enough money to complete his college degree through a correspondence course. Again with Sisulu's help, Mandela later found a job in a white law firm, where he worked while studying law part-time at the University of Witwatersrand.

ANC leader Oliver Tambo and his wife, Adelaide, enjoy a turn on the dance floor. Former classmates in college, Mandela and Tambo helped to found the ANC Youth League in 1943. They planned to use militant protest methods to demand full citizenship rights for blacks.

While in school, Mandela met Evelyn Ntoko Mase, a young nurse to whom he was attracted because of her quiet, soft-spoken manners and energetic dedication to her work. After a brief courtship, they married and moved into a small home in Orlando Township, part of the area outside Johannesburg known as Soweto (an acronym for Southwest Townships). Then a son was born, and Mandela spent most of his evenings at home with Evelyn, studying or helping to care for the baby, whom they named Thembi. Those quiet days in Soweto gave no hint of the turbulent times ahead.

Despite work, school, and his family responsibilities, Mandela still found time to become politically active again. Walter Sisulu was a member of the African National Congress, the leading black political group in South Africa, and he persuaded Mandela to join the organization. Founded in 1912 by a diverse group of black lawyers, journalists, teachers, and chiefs, the ANC originally sought to end segregation. Said one of the founders, "We were dreaming . . . of the day when Africans would sit in Parliament and would be able to buy land."

In the first decades of its existence, the ANC's protests were limited to campaigns, lobbying efforts, and occasional peaceful demonstrations and mass meetings. A passive, moderate organization known for its polite yet ineffectual leadership, the ANC was mostly ignored by both the white government and the apathetic black masses.

By the late 1930s, the ANC was nearly defunct. Dr. A. B. Xuma, named ANC president in December 1940, revitalized a number of local branches, but he too was opposed to any kind of militancy or mass demonstrations.

Barely three years later, however, a new generation of young political activists attacked the ANC leadership because of its compromises and indecision and charged that the organization had become a "body of gentlemen with clean hands." An extraordinary group of young men, including Mandela, Sisulu, Oliver Tambo (Mandela's friend from Fort Hare College), and a young lawyer named Anton Lembede formed an ANC Youth League in late 1943. The group hoped to galvanize the ANC into militant action and mass protest against the white regime, for they were convinced that only the experience of struggle against their oppressors could help erase the feelings of inferiority that Africans had developed after years of oppression. The league vowed to become the "brain trust and power station of the spirit of African nationalism." Indeed, its militant philosophy was a forerunner of the nationalism that swept Africa after World War II.

In September 1944, the Youth League elected Lembede as president; Mandela, Tambo, and Sisulu were appointed to the executive committee. Branches of the league sprang up across the country. Recalling this remarkable time, Oliver Tambo said: "We were never really young. There were no dances, hardly a cinema, but meetings, discussions, every night, every weekend." The league's members were convinced that they were the wave of the future that would bring freedom and equality to all Africans.

A new mood of defiance did appear to be sweeping South Africa. The rapid industrial expansion of the economy during the war brought unprecedented

Indian political leader Mahatma Gandhi sits in front of his law office in Johannesburg in 1895. While working as a lawyer defending the civil rights of South Africa's large Indian population, he developed his ideas for using nonviolent resistance methods to protest against unfair laws.

A comparison of this photo depicting the living conditions of black workers in the 1950s with the 1985 picture at right shows what little change has occurred in 30 years. In 1946 more than 70,000 black miners went on strike to protest these awful conditions, but the protest was brutally suppressed by the police.

unrest. In 1944, a series of spontaneous protests and boycotts erupted against the hated pass laws. In 1946, the South African Indian Congress, under the youthful leadership of Ismail Meer and J. N. Singh, fellow law students of Mandela, began a campaign of civil disobedience against the so-called Ghetto Bill, which forced Indians to live in certain areas.

The Indian Congress had been founded in 1894 by Mohandas K. Gandhi, who had spent 20 years in South Africa developing his strategy of effecting wide-scale social change through peaceful noncooperation. Using the tactics pioneered by Gandhi, the Indian Congress organized nonviolent protests, boycotts, and marches against apartheid. Mandela, a firsthand witness to the protests, was deeply impressed by the Indian activists' courage and enthusiasm. Two years later, the ANC Youth League would adopt many of those same tactics for their own purposes.

The other critical protest of 1946 came in August, when more than 70,000 black miners went on strike for better wages. The largest walkout in South Africa's history, the strike brought a harsh response from the government. Gold was the country's most important economic resource, and the white government could not afford a prolonged strike that could jeopardize the booming economy. Police and army units completely sealed off the miners' compounds, cutting off all food and water supplies. The police then raided the strikers' headquarters and barracks, arrested the leaders, and savagely attacked protesters who refused to return to work. The brutality crippled the strike, which ended within a week, but the entire incident was a tremendous lesson for the Youth Leaguers. They were convinced that if the ANC could harness the awesome power of the black working class, they would have a powerful weapon for social change.

The year 1948 was a critical point in South Africa's history. In the electoral contests of that year, the National party swept into power by promising that its policy of "apartheid," or "separate development," would reinforce the existing racial segregation. The National party tightened influx controls, prevented blacks from holding skilled jobs, and broadened the powers of the central bureaucracy that regulated apartheid. New repressive legislation was designed to silence the increasingly militant black opposition and to limit the freedom of the black majority.

The Afrikaners publicized a new ideology to justify apartheid. They argued that whites and Africans differed so greatly in cultural backgrounds and "levels of civilization" that it was best for each group to develop separately. They insisted that the Africans had become divided into so many tribes, each with its own language, culture and identity, that they no longer were a single majority. By adding these ideas to the original notions of territorial separation embodied in the Natives Land Act, the Afrikaners arbitrarily divided Africans into 10 "distinct" tribes that were to live in separate "homelands" (or "Bantustans," as they were later called), which were carved from the original native reserves. The white government even envisaged granting political independence to the homelands in the indefinite future.

The Afrikaner concept of apartheid blatantly distorted South African history. Although different tribal groups had indeed developed over time, these groups were broadly similar in dialects, values and customs. Ironically, the differences among white groups (for instance, between the Afrikaners and British) were far more substantial than those among the Africans, but such contradictions were conveniently overlooked by the Afrikaners. Furthermore, the "homelands" assigned to the Africans were designed not only to foster tribal nationalism at the expense of African solidarity (the strategy was to "divide and rule") but also to provide a reservoir of cheap labor for South Africa's industries. The new apartheid regime was a serious obstacle to freedom that Mandela and the new generation of radicals would have to overcome in their fight for African equality.

> They [the Youth League] set out to "galvanize" the ANC, which they recognized was the symbol and embodiment of the Africans' will to present a united front against all forms of oppression.
> —MARY BENSON
> South African author

31

3

No Easy Walk to Freedom

While the Afrikaners were perfecting their new policies of apartheid, the Youth League activists decided the time had come to seize the leadership of the ANC. At the ANC's annual conference in 1949, the Youth League outlined a Programme of Action, which would employ new types of direct action (strikes, civil disobedience, noncooperation) against the apartheid regime. They were convinced that only mass action and militancy would persuade the authorities to meet their demands. The Programme of Action was adopted by the ANC delegates, who also chose an entirely new leadership. Dr. James Moroka, a physician from the Free State, was elected president, and Walter Sisulu secretary-general. A number of key Youth Leaguers, including Oliver Tambo, were elected to the executive committee.

We have a powerful ideology capable of capturing the imaginations of the masses. Our duty is now to carry that ideology fully to them.
—NELSON MANDELA

While Mandela developed plans for the ANC Youth League's campaign of nonviolent resistance to the newly passed apartheid laws, he steeled himself for the struggle ahead by working out in boxing gyms. He also taught fighting skills to Soweto youth, helping them to acquire the great physical stamina needed for a successful campaign.

White South African children play while their black nanny watches, and (opposite) black children play in a garbage-strewn area near their home in a township area. Because life under the apartheid system holds very limited prospects for black youth, the system is self-perpetuating.

The new leadership's first objective was to call for a one-day national work stoppage to protest the apartheid regime. However, before the ANC could organize its campaign, an ad-hoc group (that is, one formed for a specific purpose) of activists from the Communist party, the Indian Congress, and the ANC's Transvaal branch announced its own plans to sponsor a stay-at-home protest on May 1, 1950. The purpose of that May Day demonstration was to challenge the introduction of new legislation commonly known as the Suppression of Communism Acts, which outlawed the Communist party and denied individuals the right to publicly advocate social, political, or economic change in South Africa. The organizers of the protest feared that the new law, if passed, could be used to achieve widespread repression of the entire South African freedom movement.

Mandela, Sisulu, and the other Youth League members were furious with the May Day organizers for disrupting their plans to call a work stoppage, and they spoke out against the Communist party. The league was vehemently anticommunist, and believed that Africans were oppressed not because of their class status, as the Communists claimed, but because of their race. Creating hostility between workers and capitalists, they believed, could only hamper the effort to unite all South Africans, regardless of race, against the apartheid government. "It is clear that the exotic plant of communism," wrote the young Nelson Mandela, "cannot flourish on African soil."

The Youth Leaguers also feared that the cause of African liberation would be irreparably damaged if whites (many of the leading Communist activists were white) took over the leadership of the protests. Although the ANC had always been traditionally nonracist and indeed had cooperated with whites, blacks, and Indians in multiracial actions, the Youth Leaguers believed blacks had to struggle separately for their own freedom.

Despite active Youth League opposition and strong government pressure, however, the May 1 strike was a success. In the country's largest cities, more than half the Africans stayed home, and protesters demonstrated throughout the country. Tragedy struck in Johannesburg, however; 19 Africans were killed there when police broke up meetings and demonstrations. "That day," said Mandela, "was a turning point in my life, both in understanding through firsthand experience the ruthlessness of the police, and in being deeply impressed by the support African workers had given to the May Day call."

In the days following the protest, ANC Youth Leaguers joined with the Communist party and Indian Congress in demonstrations of mourning for the dead protesters. The ANC executive committee announced a new stay-at-home demonstration for June 26 to protest the police brutality. This time, the ANC purposely sought the cooperation of the Indian Congress and the Communist party; Youth Leaguers met with both groups to iron out their differences. Mandela and the Youth League activists had gradually realized that their African exclusivism had become self-defeating. The government was suppressing not only Communists and left-wing activists but all apartheid opponents; as a result, the African liberation struggle was in danger of being crushed in its infancy. In addition, the weeks of

A police patrol marches through a black township area. In 1949, Mandela and the other members of the Youth League issued their Programme of Action, a blueprint for a democratic, multiracial state. Meanwhile, the white authorities stepped up efforts to drive blacks from the townships.

close cooperation with the other groups had convinced Mandela that the ANC needed to construct a broad multiracial alliance in order to fight the apartheid regime successfully.

Walter Sisulu from the ANC and Yusuf Chachalia from the Indian Congress were co-chairmen of the June 26 protest; Mandela was the daily coordinator. Despite only two weeks of preparation, the strike achieved remarkable results. In Johannesburg, despite incredible police intimidation, nearly three-quarters of African workers stayed at home. In Durban, Indian shopkeepers closed their stores for the day and most workers honored the strike.

Early in 1951, Mandela, recently elected national president of the Youth League, met with Sisulu, Tambo, and other ANC militants to discuss how they could build on the achievements of the protest. They were now fully committed to involving all races and political groups in future campaigns. At the ANC's conference in December 1951, the delegates approved a proposal for a new round of protests that would begin in April of the following year. The ANC demanded that unless the government repealed several apartheid laws, including the pass laws and the Suppression of Communism Act, the Congress would begin demonstrations deliberately to violate these laws. ANC president Moroka spoke of enrolling 10,000 volunteers in the nonviolent protests.

When Mandela was asked to lead what was called the Defiance Campaign as national volunteer-in-chief, he immediately toured the country to recruit volunteers. Night after night, on street corners in Durban and Johannesburg or in dilapidated homes in the black townships of Soweto and New Brighton, he preached his message of hope to the African masses. Although Africans had been the daily recipients of violence for countless years, Mandela told his fellow blacks that they must be willing to accept suffering without retaliation. He warned them that nonviolence would require tremendous courage and determination in the face of violent provocation by the police, but he promised that the tactic would bring an end to their oppression. Mandela was a natural leader of the masses; his passionate words seemed to inspire courage and confidence in everyone he met.

A black man defies the apartheid system by sitting on a "whites-only" bench in 1970. The fine for such behavior was $20 or 20 days in jail.

Demonstrators parade through the streets during the beginning of the Defiance Campaign, on June 26, 1952. After Mandela was elected president of the Youth League, he traveled around the country in search of volunteers for the campaign's nonviolent protests.

On the morning of June 26, 1952, in the New Brighton township of Port Elizabeth, the first group of volunteers inaugurated the Defiance Campaign by singing freedom songs and chanting slogans. Years before the American civil rights movement, the Africans marched through the "Europeans Only" entrance to the railroad station, where they were arrested by the waiting police. That night in Johannesburg, Mandela, Sisulu, and 50 volunteers were arrested for violating the 11:00 P.M. curfew.

Mandela's first prison experience was shocking. One of the volunteers broke his ankle after a guard pushed him downstairs, and when Mandela protested, the policeman beat him with his nightstick. Undaunted, Mandela demanded that a doctor be summoned to help the man. He was told that it was too late at night to request such assistance, but to ask again on the following day if he wished and the matter would be considered. The injured volunteer spent the night in agony.

In the weeks that followed, the Defiance Campaign spread through the rest of the country. The government was quick to retaliate; incidents took place in Cape Town, Durban, and the smaller towns in eastern Cape Province. More than 150 volunteers were arrested by the end of June; by August, the figure had risen to 2,015. Not even the arrest at ANC headquarters of many campaign leaders, including Mandela, Sisulu, and Moroka, could stem the tide of protest. An additional 2,060 volunteers were jailed in September; another 2,000 the following month. By the campaign's end in December, more than 8,000 had been imprisoned.

Nelson Mandela and several other members of the ANC leadership were brought to trial on December 2 under the Suppression of Communism Act. More than 50 of the ANC's ablest organizers and leaders were banned from participation in the Congress. Mandela received the most severe punishment: he was prohibited from traveling outside Johannesburg for the next two years and banned from attending political meetings. (Banning orders, widely issued from 1952 on, could prohibit an individual for a certain number of years from participating in a variety of activities.)

The Defiance Campaign failed to compel the South African government to repeal any of its laws. Rather, the government moved relentlessly to further entrench and expand apartheid. On the other hand, the campaign radicalized thousands of Africans and was a remarkably successful demonstration of the potential power of the African masses. The ANC had been transformed into a genuine mass movement; by the end of 1952, its membership had grown from 20,000 to some 100,000.

Because of his travel restrictions, Nelson Mandela was unable to attend the annual ANC Transvaal Conference, but he sent a written message to the delegates. The campaign had, he said, "inspired and aroused our people from a conquered and servile community of 'yes-men' to a militant and uncompromising band of comrades in arms." Yet there was still a long road to travel, he cautioned. "There is no easy walk to freedom anywhere," he wrote, quoting the words of India's prime minister Jawaharlal Nehru, "and many of us will have to pass through the valley of the shadow of death again and again before we reach the mountaintop of our desires."

Mandela (right) and Indian Congress president Yusuf Dadoo are mobbed by supporters shortly before they were arrested during the Defiance Campaign. While in jail, Mandela had his first experience with the savage treatment that blacks received from white prison guards.

4

A Partner in Struggle

The brass plate on the door read "Mandela and Tambo"; every morning, long before the law office opened, the corridor was filled with clients waiting patiently for help. Because they were forbidden to engage in political activities, the two ANC activists had set up a law firm in a decrepit building in the Indian section of Johannesburg. Peasant families traveled long distances from the countryside to seek help with problems such as recovering land that generations of their forefathers had worked. The 2 men worked 15 hours a day defending clients accused of various violations of the apartheid laws.

During this period, life for Mandela was a constant hardship. Undercover police followed him everywhere. He had to limit his contact with political associates, and many of his friends were warned by the police to stay away from him or risk imprisonment. Mandela wrote, "I was made, by the law, a criminal, not because of what I had done, but because of what I thought, because of my conscience."

We became aware of the fact that as attorneys we often dealt with officials whose competence and attainments were no higher than ours, but whose superior position was maintained and protected by a white skin.
—NELSON MANDELA

Mandela and his second wife, Winnie, pose for their wedding picture in June 1958. Completely devoted to the black nationalist cause, Mandela found little time for family life. His marriage to Winnie Madikizela, however, proved to be a sustaining force in his long, hard struggle against the apartheid system.

After being released from prison in 1952, Mandela was hounded by the police wherever he traveled. Banned from attending political meetings, he and Oliver Tambo formed a law practice and gave legal advice to people who had been charged with violating apartheid regulations.

The unremitting pressures gradually undermined Mandela's personal life. He and Evelyn had three children: two boys, Thembi and Nakgatho, and a daughter, Makawize. Evelyn, who longed for a normal family life with her husband, finally moved to Natal with the children to begin her studies as a midwife. A few months later, she sadly informed Mandela that she would not be returning, saying that she was unwilling to sacrifice her personal happiness for his political goals. Later, in 1957, the couple was divorced.

By 1954, much of the ANC's momentum seemed to have dissipated. The government bans and police intimidation and repression had crippled the Congress. Mandela, Sisulu, and the entire membership of the ANC's executive committee had been forced to resign, and although they continued to attend meetings and participate in policy decisions behind the scenes, inexperienced activists had taken over their leadership positions. Lacking money to subsidize a large, full-time staff, the leaders worked long hours for meager compensation. In addition, building a potential following in a desperately poor and illiterate population was extraordinarily difficult.

Although everyone in the ANC agreed that the first priority was to mobilize and build a mass movement, there were significant disagreements about how to do this. Many ANC leaders wanted to continue the old tactics of putting nonviolent pressure on the white government through popular campaigns and public demonstrations. Mandela, however, argued that the present situation had drastically changed since 1952 and that "new forms" of political struggle were required. Thus, in late 1953, he proposed a new strategy — called the M-Plan in his honor — to create a revitalized mass base for the African National Congress. He suggested forming a grass-roots, nationwide network of street committees, small groups of activists organized by neighborhood. Each block organization would visit neighbors' homes to recruit new ANC members on a one-to-one basis. These local groups would be linked to the national organization, which would issue all major policy statements and decisions.

Although Mandela insisted the ANC would continue to work openly and nonviolently, he believed the grass-roots committees, by working in a more discreet and disciplined manner, could better withstand government attacks and intimidation than the current, loosely constituted ANC. Mandela seemed to be implying the necessity of maintaining an effective organization should the ANC ever be driven underground by the apartheid regime. As it happened, the plan would eventually be implemented in response to governmental oppression; however, for the present, the M-Plan was largely ignored.

In 1954 a new organization, the Congress Alliance, was formed from the groups opposing apartheid: the ANC, the Indian Congress, the Congress of Trade Unions, and the Congress of Democrats, a small group of white dissidents. In order to help draft a "freedom charter," the Alliance asked people in cities and villages across South Africa what they would do if they could make the laws. Thousands of suggestions poured in, advocating higher wages, decent education and housing, and an end to the pass laws and other discriminatory policies.

Chief Lutuli, the future ANC president, proclaimed that nothing in the history of South Africa "quite caught the popular imagination as the Congress of the People." On June 25, 1955, about 3,000 delegates journeyed to a private athletic field a short distance from Johannesburg to begin the Congress. Historian Anthony Sampson described the diverse, multiracial audience: "Large African grandmothers wearing Congress skirts, Congress blouses. . . . young Indian women with glistening saris and shawls embroidered with Congress colors. . . . grey old African men, with walking sticks and Congress arm bands. . . . " The delegates were happy and festive, singing and dancing throughout the day and evening.

The Freedom Charter, which had been written on the eve of the Congress, was read to the delegates in English, Sesotha, and Xhosa. Its historic first lines began, "We the people of South Africa declare for all our country and the world to know, that South Africa belongs to all who live in it, black and

Mandela enjoys a happy moment with Thembi, one of his two sons by his first wife, Evelyn. Mandela's first marriage had broken up under the strains imposed upon it by his political work. Thembi later died tragically in an automobile accident.

A picture of ANC president Chief Albert Lutuli looms over a crowd at an anti-apartheid meeting. Although Lutuli and Mandela were banned from attending ANC meetings, both risked arrest on numerous occasions to lecture at recruitment gatherings.

white, and that no government can justly claim authority unless it is based on the will of all the people." Each section of the charter was adopted by the acclamation of the crowd. On the second day, armed security police mounted the platform and confiscated all documents, papers, and banners. Despite the interference, the meeting adjourned quietly. The meeting of the Congress marked the first time in South Africa's history that such a large multiracial group had ever publicly asserted its opposition to the apartheid regime.

The most historically significant event of the Congress was the public announcement of the Freedom Charter. This document was destined to become an enduring political testament of the liberation movement in South Africa; indeed, the charter would be adopted as a political platform by apartheid opponents 30 years later. The declaration was not a blueprint for a socialist state, as the Afrikaners have consistently asserted; instead, it envisaged an end to all apartheid legislation and the creation of a democratic society offering political and human rights for all, regardless of race. Some vague radical promises were made to nationalize the mineral industries and banks, but such actions have been implemented by socialist and nonsocialist governments alike, in the West as well as in Africa. Yet Nelson Mandela correctly argued that the charter was "a revolutionary document precisely because the changes it envisages cannot be won without breaking up the economic and political setup of present South Africa." The simple demands for democratic freedoms were, in South Africa, revolutionary challenges to the unjust system of white supremacy.

After the Congress, rumors spread that a massive crackdown by the government was imminent. The police raided ANC offices and seized vast numbers of documents and papers in preparation for a major prosecution. On December 5, 1956, in the early hours of the morning, police charged 156 persons, including Mandela, Sisulu, Tambo, and Chief Lutuli, with high treason. The state claimed they were members of "a countrywide conspiracy, inspired by international communism, to overthrow the state by violence." Mandela and the others insisted that their methods had been nonviolent and their aims democratic, and that they were on trial because of their ideas.

During a recess in the treason-trial proceedings in 1957, Mandela was eating at a Greek restaurant in downtown Johannesburg when Oliver Tambo and his fianceé Adelaide Tsukudu came in. Tsukudu insisted that Mandela meet a friend of hers who was waiting in their car. In spite of his protests that he was too busy with work, she escorted him outside and introduced him to a strikingly beautiful young woman named Winnie Madikizela — the future Winnie Mandela.

Winnie Madikizela's African name, Nomzamo (which in Xhosa means someone who will go through many trials), was as prophetic as her future husband's (stirring up trouble) had been. She was born in a tiny village in the Transkei, in the southeast, on September 26, 1934, the fifth child of Columbus and Gertrude Madikizela, both of whom were teachers in the local school district. Her father was constantly fighting with the white authorities to improve the overcrowded, ill-equipped conditions in his school. In an area where tribal dress was commonplace, he always wore a suit, and he had an imposing air of authority. Gertrude, who was deeply religious, often required Winnie and the other children to pray two or three times a day. When Winnie was almost nine, her mother died, and

> *I became aware at an early age that the whites felt superior to us. And I could see how shabby my father looked in comparison to the white teachers. That hurts your pride when you are a child.*
> —WINNIE MANDELA
> on her childhood

Holding signs that protest the Bantu Education Act and other discriminatory laws, delegates gather for the first Congress Alliance meeting in June 1955. Mandela was barred from attending the multiracial conference of antiapartheid groups, but he sent the delegates an inspiring message of support.

Columbus decided not to send the children to live with relatives, as was tribal custom, but to raise them himself. Each child was given responsibility for a specific household chore, and the Madikizela children became mature and self-assured at a very young age.

A boisterous tomboy, Winnie was her father's favorite because of her intelligence. When two Afrikaner inspectors asked to quiz one of Madikizela's students, the eight-year-old Winnie confidently answered all their questions without a single mistake. Just as Nelson Mandela had learned about his heroic ancestors at the tribal elders' campfires, Winnie learned about South Africa's troubled past from her father. Columbus Madikizela told his students of the glorious resistance of the Xhosa warriors against the Afrikaners who had stolen their land, and as she listened to these stories, Winnie developed a fierce resentment against injustice.

Winnie's strong academic record enabled her to attend secondary school in nearby Bizana — a milestone not only because it made possible her first trip outside her village but also because, for the first time in her life, she was able to wear shoes. The flair for stylish clothing she exhibited later in life probably can be traced to the thrill she felt dressing up for that first day of school.

In Bizana, Winnie also received her first insight into the harsh realities of apartheid. Winnie Mandela's biographer Nancy Harrison tells of Winnie's experience at a white-owned store, which was jammed with African tribesmen who had made the long journey into town to purchase supplies. Winnie and her father were shopping; in one corner, a farmer and his wife were trying to quiet their baby, who was screaming uncontrollably. Suddenly the white teenager who was checking the Madikizelas' order began raging at the family, kicking over their belongings, and ordering them out of the store, shouting that he would not have any *kaffirs* (a derogatory term for Africans) disturbing the peace. Not a single black in the store raised a voice in the family's defense; even Winnie's father, who had always taught the importance of fighting injustice, looked away and kept silent. Later Winnie realized that speaking up would only have made matters worse, but at the time, the 13-year-old girl was extremely distressed.

Winnie was able to attend Shawbury High School, a prestigious college preparatory institution, because of financial sacrifices her father made on her behalf. She was at Shawbury during the height of the 1952 Defiance Campaign; at night, the dormitory was alive with freedom songs about the legendary Nelson Mandela, who was widely regarded as the ANC's brightest young leader. Student activists at Shawbury, following the ANC's example, decided to defy authority and go on strike against the poor facilities and inadequate housing at the school. Photographs of young black girls in gym shorts holding protest signs immediately appeared on the front pages of all the white newspapers. Although sympathetic to the cause, Winnie chose not to join the strike, for she did not want to jeopardize her graduation and risk disappointing her father. Her fears were not unfounded — the white authorities expelled most of the protesters — but it was one of the few occasions in her life when personal concerns took precedence over political commitment.

At 16, Winnie enrolled in the Hofsmyer School in Johannesburg to begin training as a social worker. She lived in a hostel for black nurses, teachers, and students; it was there that she became friendly with a young black nurse named Adelaide Tsukudu.

In the City of Gold, Winnie was shocked by the stark contrast between the splendor of the glamorous white districts and the wretched poverty of the black population. She wrote long letters to her father about the appalling conditions in the ghettos. Columbus Madikizela wrote back to remind her that her studies should be her first priority and that, in any case, political activism was not appropriate behavior for a young woman. Thus, although Winnie's school was gripped by the political fervor of the early 1950s, she remained aloof from political affairs and did some modeling for African magazines.

During one of her vacations, Winnie went back to visit her family. Quite by accident she learned from an elderly woman that her father had arranged for her to marry the son of a local chieftain. Although

Young demonstrators in Durban, South Africa, hold a rally in support of the Congress Alliance's Freedom Charter. In a speech in praise of the document's condemnation of racism, Mandela stated that the adoption of the charter was "an event of major significance in the life of this country."

tribal marriages traditionally were arranged by parents for their children, Winnie, who loved her exciting life in Johannesburg, was shocked that her father would try to impose these customs on her. She knew her father would not undo the arrangements, however, so she rushed back to Johannesburg and wrote her father a letter telling him that she could not accept his plans.

Upon graduating from the Hofsmyer School, Winnie was forced to make another difficult choice. She won a scholarship to study for an advanced degree in sociology in the United States. At the same time, Baragwanath Hospital in Soweto asked her to become the first black medical social worker in South Africa. She decided to stay—and never regretted it.

Winnie Madikizela had been working in the hospital only a short time before her fateful meeting with Nelson Mandela. Although Nelson had seemed slightly aloof when they first met, he called Winnie the next afternoon to invite her to dinner that evening. Winnie had been awestruck at meeting the famous man and now felt terribly nervous about the night ahead. But Nelson immediately put her at ease with his joking manner, and her anxiety quickly faded. At dinner, Nelson talked about the upcoming treason trial and described the uphill battle the defendants faced in order to win an acquittal. Winnie was amazed by Nelson's confidence and optimism — especially because she knew that he was likely to be given a long prison sentence if convicted. Later the two walked through the countryside and exchanged stories of their lives in the Transkei.

Soon Nelson and Winnie began meeting every day. In some ways, the well-known, worldly, 38-year-old man and the 22-year-old woman may have seemed an unlikely couple, but they were very much in love. Theirs was hardly a whirlwind romantic courtship, however. Mandela was busy night and day with politics, and Winnie often accompanied him to ANC meetings just so they could spend time together. "He didn't belong to me. He was the people's man," Winnie once said. "I never had the dreams of a young girl falling head over heels with a Prince Charming. There was no time for that."

When Nelson proposed, he told Winnie how deeply he loved her but warned that she would face tremendous hardships if they married. They could never have a normal family life because of constant police harassment; she might face many years alone if he received a long prison sentence. Moreover, he made it clear that the political struggle always would come first, even before his personal feelings for her. Winnie told Nelson that she completely believed in his dream; together they pledged that they would forge an unshakable commitment to the fight for freedom.

Nelson and Winnie were married in the Methodist church in Bizana on June 14, 1958. Because of Nelson's banning restrictions, the couple had to return to Johannesburg before they could cut the wedding cake at the bridegroom's home. Winnie Mandela still has the cake today, as she awaits her husband's release from prison. As Nancy Harrison recounts, "Miraculously and perhaps symbolically, the cake has never crumbled away" in the almost 30 years since their wedding.

Dressed in an ANC uniform, Winnie Mandela leads a funeral procession that was held in the midst of the government's treason trials of Mandela and 155 other opponents of apartheid. A staunch advocate of her husband's causes, Winnie was appointed to the executive committee of the ANC's Women's League.

5

The Struggle Is My Life

The treason trial reconvened on August 1, 1958. The government, which had begun prosecuting the case a year and a half earlier, continued to overwhelm the court with endless exhibits and evidence against the defendants. The time and expense needed to mount the defense immobilized the ANC leadership, but the trial also gave a tremendous boost to the ANC's prestige throughout the country.

The trial completely overshadowed the life of the Mandela household. Their small home in the Orlando West township of Soweto was alive with meetings at all hours. Nelson left home every morning for the trial in Pretoria and returned exhausted late in the evening, with barely enough time to eat and shower before people started pouring in for late-night strategy sessions. "Even at that stage, life with him was a life without him," said Winnie. "He did not ever pretend that I would have some special claim to his time."

If you strip men of each and every right, you can only organize them into a Force to be reckoned with. The government is actually organizing the masses of us.
—WINNIE MANDELA

In the face of constant police harassment, the ANC's supporters turned out in throngs to cheer on Mandela, Sisulu, and other resistance leaders who were charged with treason. The trial, which lasted from December 1956 to March 1961, mobilized great enthusiasm for the black nationalist movement.

A Johannesburg resident displays the passbook that he is required to carry with him at all times. After demonstrating against the pass laws in October 1958, Winnie Mandela was arrested and beaten, nearly suffering a miscarriage.

When the apartheid regime announced that the pass laws would become mandatory for black women as well as men, the Women's League of the ANC called for a mass demonstration. Winnie, who was pregnant with her first child, was arrested along with 1,200 other female protestors and thrown into prison. In the process she received several blows and began to hemorrhage. Luckily for Winnie, Albertina Sisulu, Walter Sisulu's wife, also had been arrested; an experienced midwife, she cared for Winnie and prevented her having a miscarriage. Two weeks later, the prisoners were released, but to Winnie's dismay she found she had been fired from her hospital job. She had only been married a short time, but already her personal life had been dramatically affected by the liberation struggle.

In 1960, there was a widespread sense among Africans that the new decade marked a new era in South Africa. Blacks were inspired because an unprecedented number of African states had won their independence from Western colonial control, and protests continued against the regime in Johannesburg and the rural areas. The treason trial kept the African National Congress in the public eye, and its popularity had never been greater. When British Prime Minister Harold Macmillan spoke before the South African parliament in Cape Town, he cautioned that the "winds of change" were sweeping through the land.

For a time, the winds of change blew with hurricane force. In February 1960 a militant nationalist group, the Pan-Africanist Congress (PAC), led by Robert Sobukwe, announced the beginning of a pass-law resistance campaign scheduled for March 21 — 10 days before protests planned by the ANC were slated to start. The PAC, which had seceded from the ANC in 1959 because they disagreed with the Congress's commitment to multiracialism and felt the leaders of the ANC had not been sufficiently daring, now proposed that Africans should stop carrying their passes, risk mass arrests, and stop working until the pass laws were abolished.

The massacre of peaceful demonstrators by police in the Sharpeville township on March 21, 1960, focused world attention on the brutality of South Africa's racist policies. To protest the violence against blacks, the ANC organized a national day of mourning and a series of strikes and passbook-burning demonstrations.

A week after the massacre of blacks in the Sharpeville and Langa townships, more than 30,000 marchers in Cape Town joined in an outcry against racial oppression. Announcing a state of emergency, the government outlawed the ANC and jailed Mandela and other resistance leaders.

On the morning of March 21, 1960, Sobukwe and other top PAC members publicly burned their passes and were quickly arrested. The turnout in Johannesburg was negligible, but to the south, a crowd of 10,000 protestors gathered in the Sharpeville township outside the city of Vereeniging. The demonstrators were well mannered and cheerful, but suddenly the police panicked and opened fire on the unarmed crowd. People screamed and fled — yet the firing continued for another 30 seconds. Sixty-seven Africans, including 8 women and 10 children, were killed; most had been shot in the back as they fled. That same evening, the police again fired on a peaceful crowd in the Cape Town township of Langa, killing 14 and wounding countless others.

The Sharpeville massacre produced an unprecedented political crisis in South Africa. Horrifying photos of the murders appeared in newspapers throughout the world and sparked a furious outcry of international condemnation. The United Nations Security Council spoke out on South African affairs for the first time. It unanimously passed a resolution denouncing the killings and urging the initiation of "measures aimed at bringing about racial harmony and equality."

The South African government had always contemptuously dismissed any "outside interference," but the repercussions from the Sharpeville massacre were too serious to be ignored. South Africa's currency, the rand, dropped precipitously on international financial markets amid widespread speculation that future foreign investment, the lifeblood of the apartheid economy, might stop. In an attempt to sway international opinion and perhaps deflate further protests at home, the government shrewdly announced on March 26 that arrests for pass-law violations would be temporarily suspended. At the same time, it acted decisively to prevent further demonstrations, sending armored vehicles to patrol the townships, canceling police leaves, and mobilizing citizen reserves.

In spite of the mighty South African security apparatus, the African rebellion continued to spread. Serious rioting erupted in Johannesburg, and a spontaneous strike in Cape Town crippled the city's docks and factories. On March 26, Chief Lutuli, the ANC president, publicly burned his passbook and encouraged Africans to follow his lead. On March 28 a crowd of more than 50,000 crammed into Langa township for the funerals of the Sharpeville victims. ANC and Pan-Africanist Congress orators urged that the protests and strikes continue until the apartheid policies were dismantled. It appeared that the "day of reckoning between the forces of freedom and those of reaction," which Nelson Mandela had predicted eight years earlier, had finally become unavoidable.

On March 30, the white government proclaimed a nationwide state of emergency, which granted the police broad powers to arrest and detain indefinitely anyone suspected of opposition activities or sympathies. That same day, a dramatic procession of 30,000 blacks, led by a 23-year-old PAC activist named Philip Kgosana, marched to the center of the legislative capital of Cape Town, stopping 3 blocks from the parliament. The marchers were halted by heavily armed police and army units; helicopters flew overhead intimidatingly. Such a spirited mass demonstration by Africans in the heart of a South

African city was completely unprecedented. No one was sure what would happen. Kgosana demanded to see the minister of justice; the police commander said a meeting would be held only if the marchers dispersed and returned to their homes. Kgosana agreed, and the marchers went quietly back to the townships. When Kgosana returned later that evening for the promised interview, he was arrested and placed in detention under the new state of emergency.

"A decisive historical moment had come and passed by," wrote historian Gail Gerhart, "leaving whites shaken but still firmly in control." Indeed, many historians have argued that if the Cape Town march had escalated into another violent incident like Sharpeville, it would have precipitated a revolutionary situation similar to the storming of the Bastille in France or the assault on the Winter Palace in Russia in 1905. If anything, the incident and its aftermath dramatically illustrated the true imbalance of power in the country. Army troops cordoned off the black townships of Cape Town and brutally crushed the strike in three days. Thousands of Africans were arrested around the country; Mandela and the other treason-trial defendants were seized again and jailed. On April 8, the government outlawed the ANC and PAC and reinstated the pass laws.

Mandela (second from right) and other treason trial defendants file into court. The long hours Mandela spent preparing the defense's case finally led to victory. In March 1961, the presiding judge declared all of the accused not guilty, setting off wild celebrations in the black community.

The ANC leaders had woefully underestimated the ruthlessness of the white regime and were unprepared for the massive government crackdown. Oliver Tambo secretly left to establish an ANC organization in exile, but most of the leading organizers and activists of the ANC were arrested in the nationwide police sweeps. The ANC was unable to mount any kind of organized resistance and could only issue ineffectual statements denouncing the white government. Yet despite the setbacks the freedom movement suffered in those first months of 1960, the Sharpeville incident shook the foundations of white supremacy to the core.

After Sharpeville, the treason trial, which had begun in late 1956, once again resumed in Pretoria. Mandela remained in detention in abominable conditions, unable to see Winnie or his newborn daughter, Zeni. The government continued to insist that the ANC was part of an international communist conspiracy that advocated the violent overthrow of the South African regime.

In August 1960, the state began its lengthy cross-examination of Mandela, scrutinizing his speeches and writings and interrogating him about the ANC's past policies, until more than 400 pages of the official trial record had been filled. Mandela defended the Defiance Campaign and Congress Alliance as nonviolent movements and repeated his belief that the ANC's strategy of civil disobedience would one day bring freedom to all Africans. He denied that the ANC represented any threat to the whites. His defense was brilliant, and it brought him not only international fame but increased stature within the ANC as well. Nelson Mandela was now universally regarded as the ANC's most impressive and capable leader.

On March 27, 1961, the defense was still in the midst of its arguments when, surprisingly, the chief judge announced that the court was returning a verdict of not guilty and that the defendants were free to go. Spectators cheered wildly and sang the African national anthem, "Nkosi Sikelel Afrika" (God Bless Africa). When the Mandelas returned

> *My colleagues and I . . . decided that we would not obey the decree outlawing [the African National] Congress. We believed it was our duty to preserve this organization which has been built up with almost fifty years of unremitting toil.*
> —NELSON MANDELA
> on the M-Plan

Mandela and Winnie embrace in celebration of the government's rescinding of the state-of-emergency orders and Mandela's release from jail in August 1960. In court testimony, Mandela stated that the ANC was not an opponent of the white community but rather of unjust laws.

home for a victory celebration, Nelson asked Winnie to pack his suitcase. He had made plans to go away for a long time in order to carry on his work in a new way. He told her that he would ask friends to look after her and that he would be in touch. Winnie's eyes were brimming with tears as she embraced Nelson for the last time.

Mandela next appeared in the eastern South African city of Pietermaritzburg as the keynote speaker at the All-In-Africa Conference. With his unerring instinct for the appropriate theatrical gesture, he mounted the platform barefoot to symbolize that he was first and foremost a leader who represented the common people. Every sentence of his inspiring address was greeted with cheers and applause. He called on Africans to refuse to cooperate unless the government convened a multiracial national convention to draft a new democratic constitution for South Africa. Mandela was unanimously elected head of the National Action Council, which would organize a two-day, nationwide protest beginning on May 29, 1961, unless their demands were met. Then Mandela dramatically announced that because he could no longer operate freely in South Africa, he was going underground to wage the struggle.

The decision to continue the fight in secret was the result of a great deal of soul-searching by the ANC after the Sharpeville massacre. More than any other incident, Sharpeville demonstrated the futility of nonviolent civil disobedience. Such actions would be brutally crushed by the South African regime even though it was not yet a full-fledged police state.

Banned the year before, the ANC now proposed a new strategy, based on the M-Plan that Mandela had proposed in 1953. The organization would now reconstitute itself on a grass-roots level; members would be recruited into secret local groups, organized street by street and house by house. Mandela, chosen to lead the new initiative, would help coordinate the new organizations and would surface periodically to appear at important public events. From now on, Mandela would "live as an outlaw" in his own land.

During the next two months, Mandela made surprise visits to key industrial areas and journeyed to the country's black townships to promote the stay-at-home strike. The apartheid government put on an extraordinary display of military might as the day drew near. Helicopters flew over African townships each night searching for public gatherings; armored cars patrolled the streets. The government used the strike as a pretext to arrest more than 10,000 Africans, who were placed in indefinite detention without trial. On May 29, 60 percent of the black workers stayed home in Johannesburg and Pretoria, but other cities had only a mediocre response. Mandela was forced to cancel the second day of the demonstration. "If the government reaction is to crush by naked force our non-violent struggle," Mandela said, "we will have to reconsider our tactics. In my mind, we are closing a chapter on this question of a non-violent policy."

A month later, Mandela, still in hiding, issued a statement that implied that the ANC was developing new tactics. He urged Africans to continue to oppose the regime. "The struggle is my life. . . . I will continue fighting for my freedom until the end of my days."

Just days after the end of the treason trial, Mandela gives an electrifying address at the All-in-Africa Conference. He announced that he was going underground to organize a grass-roots resistance movement in an armed struggle against apartheid.

6

Taking Up the Sword

By June 1961, Mandela and his colleagues had realized that the time had come to "answer violence with violence." Mandela and a small cadre of ANC veterans and members of the Communist party decided to form a new organization, Umkhonto we Sizwe (Spear of the Nation, or MK), to plan violent attacks against the apartheid regime. The decision to abandon nonviolent struggle was made, wrote Mandela, "only when all else had failed, when all channels of peaceful protest had been barred." Mandela believed that only highly responsible leadership could stop the Africans' anger from exploding into a race war.

Accordingly, the MK decided to limit its use of violence to sabotage, avoiding terrorism, guerrilla warfare, and open revolt. "Sabotage," Mandela explained, "did not involve loss of life and it offered the best hope for future race relations." The tactic would be used primarily against power plants, rail-

You must view our violence in the context of the regime's violence, which is far, far greater. Compared to what the regime has done, we are notable not for our ferocity, but for our restraint.
—OLIVER TAMBO

Winnie Mandela leads a group of women wearing national dress into the courtroom where her husband is on trial. Secretly visiting units of his newly formed Umkhonto we Sizwe (MK) resistance group, Mandela directed sabotage strikes against government facilities until his capture in 1962.

Toppled by an MK explosive charge, a power-line tower lies on its side. Choosing a violent means of protest that avoided bloodshed, Mandela believed that his sabotage campaign would alarm foreign investors and force the South African government to change its racist policies.

roads, and telephone communications; targets would be chosen to minimize the danger of injuring or killing innocent bystanders. Umkhonto hoped the attacks would frighten off foreign investors and force the Pretoria regime to reconsider its position or suffer heavy economic drain. Umkhonto organizers knew they faced an uphill battle; building a secret organization in a country riddled with informers, where blacks could arbitrarily be stopped and searched at any moment, would be monumentally difficult. The MK activists themselves faced great personal risk if they were caught: the death penalty.

Mandela was adept at evading capture. He moved around the country, constantly switching from one safe house to another, staying barely one step ahead of the huge dragnet police had set out for his capture. Mary Benson describes a close call Mandela had while waiting on a street corner in downtown Johannesburg. He was dressed as a chauffeur, complete with uniform and cap (one of his favorite disguises) when a black policeman who passed by immediately recognized him. Instead of sounding the alarm, the officer simply winked and gave Mandela the ANC salute. The press avidly reported each new escape and appearance by Mandela; they even nicknamed him the "Black Pimpernel" after the daring fictional character, the "Scarlet Pimpernel," who constantly eluded capture during the French Revolution.

The South African security police shadowed Winnie constantly, but with the help of friends and careful planning, she and Nelson were sometimes able to see each other while Nelson was underground. Winnie could never be sure when she would be contacted, and countless precautions had to be taken. A stand-in would dress in Winnie's clothing to throw off the police surveillance, for example; then Winnie would switch cars several times before being whisked away to Nelson's latest hideout.

Nelson was greatly inspired by these brief moments with Winnie and his daughters. One of his happiest family experiences began in October 1961, when Umkhonto rented a small farm in Rivonia, a suburb on the outskirts of Johannesburg. The Mandelas moved into a small cottage there, and for a while at least they lived like a real family. Winnie cooked meals for Nelson and the children, and Nelson took the girls for long walks in the garden. Indeed, their eldest daughter Zeni imagined it to be their real home, for it was the only place she could remember being with her father. Years later, she would ask Winnie, "Mommy, when are we going home to see Daddy?"

After Mandela returned to South Africa, he resumed his conferences with resistance leaders and visited his family when near Johannesburg. In August 1962, however, Winnie learned that her husband had been betrayed and captured. Three months later, he was sentenced to five years in prison with hard labor.

On December 16, 1961, the Day of the Covenant, when Afrikaners commemorated the anniversary of the defeat of the Zulus at Blood River in 1838, the MK exploded a series of small homemade bombs at symbolic targets throughout the country, hitting power stations, railroads, and government offices in Port Elizabeth and Johannesburg. The MK issued a manifesto stating that its goal was to change the government and its policies "before matters reach the desperate stage of civil war."

Mandela secretly left South Africa in January 1962 to begin a tour of independent African states. He flew first to Addis Ababa, the capital of Ethiopia, to address a conference of African liberation movements. While there, he saw his old friend and ally Oliver Tambo. Mandela hoped to receive enough assistance from African nations to provide military training for new MK recruits and scholarships for young Africans who would become the administrators and technicians of a free South Africa. Mandela was greeted enthusiastically by leaders from Algeria, Kenya, and Tanzania and even managed to visit London to meet with the head of the British Labour party. The trip was a marvelous experience. For the first time in his life, he felt like a free man. "Wherever I went," he wrote, "I was treated like a human being."

Mandela confers with Algerian army officers in June 1962. Defying government orders barring him from leaving South Africa, he visited England and then toured throughout Africa. During his travels, he tried to raise funds for the South African freedom movement.

Mandela returned to South Africa in mid-July and reported on his tour to the National High Command of Umkhonto, in Johannesburg. He then consulted with comrades in Natal and met secretly with Chief Lutuli, the ANC president, who recently had been awarded the 1961 Nobel Peace Prize.

Then what many had dreaded finally happened. On August 5, 1962, while Mandela was returning to Johannesburg, he was captured by the South African police, apparently on a tip from an informer. When Winnie found out, she called the arrest "the collapse of a political dream." She realized what a serious blow Nelson's capture was to the African cause and what a great personal loss it was for her and her family. As Winnie wrote years later, "Part of my soul went with him at that time."

Albert Lutuli accepts the 1960 Nobel Peace Prize for his efforts in behalf of racial equality. Although Lutuli did not agree with Mandela's use of armed resistance methods, the two ANC leaders remained close friends.

Chanting "*Amandla*" (power), angry demonstrators rally after Mandela, Sisulu, and seven other resistance leaders were sentenced to life in prison in June 1964. World opinion condemned the court decision as a death-blow to any hopes for free-

A series of MK attacks followed Mandela's arrest, and the South African government intensified its counterinsurgency measures against the African liberation movement. The Sabotage Act of 1962 made death the penalty for any act of sabotage against the regime. Banning restrictions also were broadened considerably: South Africans were prohibited from publishing the writings or speeches of anyone who was banned, and those who were banned were forbidden to communicate with other banned persons or to have visitors in their homes. The government also imposed house arrest on the opposition. Activists were restricted to their homes every night after sundown and throughout the weekends. South Africa had become a police state.

On October 22, 1962, the government brought Nelson Mandela to trial, charging him with inciting strikes and with leaving the country without valid travel documents. There was no direct evidence linking him with the MK, however.

In the courtroom, Nelson, dressed in traditional Thembu tribal robes, raised his fist to the spectators' gallery and shouted "Amandla" (power); the crowd answered, "Ngawethu" (to the people). Winnie wore a strikingly beautiful Xhosa dress, and when the government refused to let her continue to wear tribal attire, she came to court dressed in black, green, and yellow — the colors of the outlawed ANC.

Once again Mandela conducted his own defense and delivered a stinging indictment of the apartheid regime. He protested that he could not get a fair trial, that "equity before the law" did not hold for Africans who all their lives were denied fundamental freedoms and rights. His presentation was a searching, thoughtful commentary on his decision to become a radical. It was necessary to explain, he said, why he, an attorney, would consciously choose to violate the laws he had sworn to uphold and respect. Echoing the sentiments of the American revolutionaries, Mandela declared that he felt neither "morally nor legally obliged" to obey the laws of a government in which neither he nor his people were adequately represented.

Most important, Mandela insisted his decision had been a matter of conscience. His entire life had been dedicated to the peaceful struggle for freedom, yet the government had treated him as a dangerous animal and had tried forcibly to suppress his cause. Despite all the suffering and hardships, however, he had no regrets. "If I had my time over," he said, "I would do the same again; so would any man who dares call himself a man."

Mandela was found guilty on both counts and sentenced to 10 years of hard labor. On his last day in court, he said that he did not fear going to jail. "Not just I alone but all of us are willing to pay the penalties we may have to pay," Mandela said. "Many people in this country have paid the price before me

> *I hope to be able to indicate that this case is a trial of the aspirations of the African people, and because of that I thought it proper to conduct my own defence.*
> —NELSON MANDELA
> on his decision to represent himself during his second trial

67

and many will pay the price after me." Although saddened, Winnie Mandela expressed no surprise at the verdict and asserted: "I will continue the fight as I have in all ways done in the past. The greatest honor a people can pay to a man behind bars is to keep the freedom flame burning, to continue the fight."

Umkhonto continued its offensive after Mandela's arrest and sentencing. By the middle of 1963, almost 200 acts of sabotage had been perpetrated by MK forces. On May 11, the government passed a new 90-day detention law, which gave police the authority to detain people for repeated 90-day periods. In the next months hundreds of men and women vanished into South Africa's prisons; in September, an ANC member became the first political activist to die in prison while under interrogation.

On July 12, 1963, an anonymous tip by an informer led the police to the ANC's Rivonia farm, where they captured the leaders of the Umkhonto high command, including Walter Sisulu. Also confiscated were an immense number of incriminating documents detailing plans for sabotage and guerrilla warfare. The arrests were a catastrophic blow for the Africans; the underground movement was left virtually leaderless, and forces outside the country would be completely isolated for almost a decade.

The trial of the Rivonia defendants opened on October 9, 1963. Mandela had been added to the group of prisoners; his diary of his tour of Africa and other papers that documented his position in the MK leadership had been discovered in the raid on the Rivonia farm. The prisoners were charged with attempting violently to overthrow the government; if found guilty, they were likely to be sentenced to death. Their lawyers did not want Mandela or the others to testify, and hoped to show that the MK's policy of sabotage was designed to avoid loss of life.

Mandela, however, told their attorney Bram Fischer, "You are concerned with saving our lives. . . . Our first concern is the fulfillment of our political beliefs." They were going to confess freely to their acts of sabotage and would seek to convince the world of the justice of their case.

By incarcerating Nelson Mandela and the other freedom fighters there [Robben Island] they hoped to wipe their names from the lips of the people of South Africa, to bury them living into oblivion.
— S. R. MAC MAHARAJ
former prisonmate of
Nelson Mandela

Winnie Mandela escorts her husband's mother, Nonqaphi, into court during Mandela's trial in 1964. In his stirring defense of his right to battle violent oppression with armed civil disobedience, Mandela stated that the ANC was engaged in "a struggle for the right to live."

Mandela and the others proudly took the stand in their own defense and condemned the South African regime. On June 11, 1964, the 46-year-old Mandela was convicted and sentenced to life imprisonment on Robben Island, a maximum-security prison off the coast of Cape Town. "To most of the world," wrote the *New York Times*, "the Rivonia defendants are heroes and freedom fighters, the George Washingtons and Ben Franklins of South Africa." The words of the *Times* of London eloquently summarized the opinion of the world: "The verdict of history will be that the ultimate guilty party is the government in power."

7

Robben Island

When Nelson Mandela and his comrades landed on Robben Island, the prison guards taunted them cruelly: "You're going to die here." The gloomy, desolate place certainly did not inspire hope. The special prisoners were housed in an isolated section of the jail. A 30-foot wall separated them from all other inmates. Mandela lived in a seven-feet-square concrete cell that was furnished with only a mat, a bedroll, and two light blankets. His prison uniform consisted of cotton shorts, a khaki shirt, and a thin jacket — hardly enough to keep him warm during the cold South African nights.

Mandela and his fellow prisoners were awakened each morning at 5:00 A.M. and given half an hour for a cold shower and shave before a breakfast of tasteless porridge. The prison authorities offered Mandela a special diet, which he refused; in all his years in prison, Mandela never once used his international reputation to gain personal privileges, and he participated fully in all common duties. Moreover, although he was clearly regarded by all the prisoners as spokesman and leader, Mandela refused to encourage a cult of personality.

At the time [June 1964] Nelson's jail conditions were appalling. The food was particularly bad and there were no privileges. We had to fight for every one of those over the years.
—WINNIE MANDELA

Mandela entered prison to begin serving his life sentence in June 1964. Like other political prisoners, he was allowed only minimal contact with his family. Unable to talk to the press, he yet remained a powerful symbol of black resistance and his international stature continued to grow.

Prison life was relentlessly grim. Every day the men had to work in a limestone quarry on the far side of the island. Before their long walk began, they were paired off and chained together at the ankles. Conversation was forbidden; the only solace was a breathtaking view of Cape Town and Table Mountain in the distance. Some prisoners chiseled blocks of limestone out of the ground and loaded the huge slabs onto trucks; others had the exhausting task of crushing rocks into useless piles of dust. The blazing heat made the quarry feel like a furnace. Each night Mandela and his comrades trudged back to their cells, grotesquely caked with white lime dust. Their arms and backs aching, the prisoners ate and then collapsed onto their bunks.

Contact with the outside world was restricted. Mandela and his fellow prisoners were granted only one half-hour visit and one incoming and one outgoing letter every six months. Just before Christmas in 1964, Winnie Mandela traveled from Johannesburg to Robben Island for her first visit with her husband. The prison warden told her that she and Nelson would not be permitted to use their tribal language, Xhosa. Political issues could not be discussed; their conversations could deal only with family matters. She was not allowed to bring Nelson any presents or packages, and their daughters would not be able to see their father until they were 14 years old.

The Mandelas' visit together was sad and disconcerting. Winnie was escorted into a dim room, where a thick glass partition separated visitors from prisoners. (In all their visits together, Winnie would never have a totally clear view of her husband.) The couple was forced to communicate with headsets; they knew that if they mentioned a name or event that the authorities did not recognize, the phones would be disconnected and the visit ended. (Over time, however, the couple developed their own special language.)

The first six months after Nelson's banishment to Robben Island were extremely difficult for Winnie. She was banned from traveling outside Johannesburg and from attending political meetings, and she was allowed only a single visitor in her home at any particular moment. Most of her close friends were either in jail or had fled the country. Several years later, remembering this time, she wrote that "loneliness is . . . the most wretchedly powerful illness the body and mind can be subjected to." When she received her first letter from Nelson, she read it over and over, memorizing it, until the next one arrived six months later.

Winnie was forced to resign her job as a social worker for the Child Welfare Society, and she discovered that finding steady employment was very difficult. Each new employer received phone calls from the security police threatening all kinds of reprisals unless Winnie was fired. In some cases, she was actually hired on a Monday and let go on the same afternoon. She worked a variety of menial positions — in a furniture shop, a dry cleaners, a laundry — and for years, she and her children suffered severe economic hardships. They survived mainly because of the charity of her friends and supporters.

But far worse than these financial troubles was the unremitting police harassment and terror Winnie had to endure. Spies and informers were a regular part of her life; on several occasions, she discovered that a seemingly sympathetic journalist or apparent political supporter who had cultivated her friendship actually was employed by the security police. The police visited her house three or four times a day, followed her when she went shopping, and monitored her phone calls and visitors. One evening, Winnie was bathing her children when she noticed the silhouette of a gun in her bathroom window. Her neighbors, who always kept a close watch for intruders, spotted the man and scared him away with their shouts.

The harassment affected her children's lives, of course. Zeni and Zindzi often were petrified with fear; Winnie was frequently arrested, and the children were never sure that she would be home to greet them when they returned from school. "They knew we [Nelson and Winnie] loved them," said Winnie about her daughters, "but we were never there to express it — it was love by proxy." Winnie tried to

> *In her determination and fearlessness Winnie Mandela typifies the black women of South Africa who are the unsung heroines of a largely untold story.*
> —NANCY HARRISON
> historian

Mandela (left) and Walter Sisulu confer in the rock-breaking area of the Robben Island prison yard. Mandela combatted the prison guards' attempts to destroy the morale of black freedom fighters by organizing hunger strikes and work slowdowns to win better conditions for the inmates.

make up for the time lost as best she could, singing the children beautiful Xhosa lullabies every night before sleep and spending entire afternoons reading stories to her daughters or teaching them new games.

The children, who stayed with Winnie's friends during each separation, learned to be courageous and self-reliant at a very young age. As a teenager, Zindzi published a poem that poignantly captures those bittersweet years:

> I need a neighbor who will live a teardrop away.
> Who will open up when I knock late at night.
> I need a child who will play a smile away.
> Who will always whisper I love you to be my mommy.

No matter what the provocation or hardship, Winnie maintained a carefree, happy demeanor and encouraged the same behavior in her children. When Zindzi cried in front of a white policeman, Winnie told her, "You must never cry, because you are giving them satisfaction if you do so."

In order to protect Zeni and Zindzi from the anguish and distress of the police harassment, Winnie sent them both away to a private school in Swaziland. "It was the hardest thing for me to take as a mother," she said, "that your commitment affects those who are very dear to you."

It was around this time that Nelson Mandela waged a human rights struggle within the confines of the prison. He demanded that he and his comrades be treated as political prisoners and be given the rights and privileges their political status warranted. The prison authorities would hear only individual complaints, however, and Mandela refused to cooperate, charging that the policy was intended to isolate so-called troublemakers. He led a series of protests — hunger strikes, work stoppages, and petitions — and won for the men better food and clothing, more blankets, a prison library, and the right to exercise and communicate with each other.

Mandela was a shrewd tactician in his dealings with the prison authorities. He sought an interview with every new commanding officer, not only to size up the man but also to inform him of the prisoners' long-standing complaints. Mac Maharaj, who was imprisoned on Robben Island with Mandela for several years, recounts how one commandant tried to counteract Mandela's authority. He refused Mandela's request for an interview and immediately set out to destroy the prisoners' solidarity — suspending privileges, ruthlessly crushing protests, and placing offenders in solitary confinement.

When a commission of judges arrived at the prison to investigate charges of torture under the new commandant, they asked specifically for an interview with Mandela. The commandant asked Mandela in front of the commission if he had ever been ordered to be tortured. "No, not me personally," Mandela admitted, "but what you have been doing to some of my colleagues affects us all. You are persecuting us." The commandant screamed that Mandela would pay for his insolence. The officer was soon transferred to another post.

The government was similarly unsuccessful in its attempts to pressure Winnie Mandela to surrender the struggle. In the first years after Nelson's im-

His [Mandela's] warmth comes out in his real sense of concern for his comrades in prison. In an unobtrusive way he finds out if anybody has problems and he tries to spend time with them if they do. Although he is completely committed to the ANC his approach to all prisoners is always warm.
—S. R. MAC MAHARAJ
former prisonmate of
Nelson Mandela

The Soweto ghetto outside of Johannesburg has long been a center of black militancy. In an effort to assure imprisoned black activists that their sacrifices were not forgotten, Winnie Mandela mobilized women in Soweto to write letters to the inmates.

prisonment, Winnie was a mere novice in politics. As Winnie recalled years later, she "was just a little girl fumbling along." Anxious to dispel any notions that she was simply a "political ornament" for her husband's career, and despite the fact that she had been ordered to refrain from political activity, Winnie found ways to fight back.

She learned that ANC activists imprisoned in the city of Port Elizabeth were not allowed to contact their families in Johannesburg and that only a few had received any mail from the outside. She promptly organized a group of women in Soweto to write supportive letters to the men, and her close friend Helen Joseph, a white opponent of the regime for over 25 years, donated funds to cover all mailing expenses.

In 1969, the South African government enacted new legislation, known as the Terrorism Act, which granted the police authority to arrest anyone suspected of committing or even inspiring actions that endangered law and order. The law was so loosely defined that it gave the government free reign to detain in solitary confinement almost any opponent of the regime for an indefinite period, without trial and without access to attorneys. On May 12, 1969, Winnie Mandela and 21 other men and women became the first targets of the new law. Winnie was arrested and placed in solitary confinement in Pretoria Central Prison. She would spend the next 17 months in jail.

The first few days were the hardest. "The whole thing is calculated to destroy you, not only morally but also physically," said Winnie. She was allowed no outside contacts and talked to no one inside the prison for the first few weeks. Her minuscule cell was unbelievably filthy; she slept on a small mat on the floor and had only two urine-stained blankets to protect her from the cold. She was forced to use a tiny metal bucket both as a toilet and as a washbasin. The prison food was completely inedible — either it came uncooked or else the guards left her tray outside the cell so long that the food became infested with insects.

The worst hardship of all was the unrelenting loneliness and boredom. The light was always on in her cell, so the days and nights, indistinguishable from one another, stretched endlessly on. With nothing to read and no one to talk to, Winnie paced up and down the cell for hours to keep her sanity. At one point, she ripped apart one of her precious blankets and used the threads to make little ropes the way her grandmother had done when she was a child. When two ants wandered into her cell one morning, Winnie spent the entire day playing with them. "You cannot imagine," she said, "the joy there was in seeing a living creature."

The police began their interrogation two weeks after Winnie was imprisoned. They could not risk visible torture on such a well-known person, but they used other means to break her spirit. For five days and nights, a series of interrogators questioned Winnie around the clock in a brilliantly lit room. The police taunted her, saying she would be broken, and Winnie lost consciousness several times. As soon as she regained consciousness, the relentless questioning began again. Winnie had to be extremely careful not to incriminate her friends accidentally. At one point, the police offered to release her if she agreed to make a radio broadcast asking the ANC guerrillas to surrender their weapons. Winnie just laughed at their stupidity.

When Winnie and the other 21 defendants were finally brought to trial, they were charged with trying to revive the ANC. The prosecutor's case was amazingly flimsy: Most of the evidence had been given by witnesses who were either police informers or inmates who had been tortured until they testified against her. In February 1970, Winnie and the other defendants were declared not guilty, but as they left the courthouse they were rearrested and again placed in solitary confinement. In September, they were charged with similar offenses, but this time they were acquitted after just a three-day trial. Winnie's imprisonment had been a horrifying ordeal; now she had to try and pick up the pieces of her life.

Winnie Mandela was arrested on vague charges of inciting disorder after the government passed a broad new antiterrorism act in 1969. Withstanding torture and nearly 500 days in solitary confinement in a Pretoria prison, she refused to give up her political activities.

8

The Soweto Uprising

In a very deep sense she qualifies for the title of being 'The Mother of Black People.' I am not saying this simply because she happens to be the wife of her husband . . . but because of what she has become in her own right.
—BISHOP MANAS BUTHELEZI
President of the South African Council of Churches, on Winnie Mandela

Many of the prisoners who left prison with Winnie Mandela were permanently scarred by their experience. They retreated into their private lives and abandoned their former political commitments. Winnie Mandela, however, emerged in even higher spirits than before. "I got more liberated in prison. The physical identification with your beliefs is far more satisfying than articulating them on a platform," she wrote in *Part of My Soul*, a collection of her conversations and letters. She went on to say that ". . . the whole country is a prison for the black man — and when you are inside, you know why you are there and the people who put you there also know."

In November 1970, Winnie traveled to Robben Island for her first visit with Nelson in more than two years. "Going to Robben Island is a fantastic feeling, it's like recharging your batteries," she said. "Each time I've seen him it has been a rebuilding of my inner soul." It was an emotional meeting; both Winnie and Nelson had experienced tremendous personal anguish during their long time apart.

Black students attend class. By the 1970s, Mandela had become a hero of nearly mythic proportions to young black South Africans, most of whom had never heard him speak. Although the ANC's teachings were banned in classrooms, illicit copies of Mandela's calls for resistance to apartheid circulated throughout the townships.

FOR FREEDOM WE SHALL
LAY DOWN OUR LIVES.
THE STRUGGLE CONTINUES.

South African resistance groups were strongly influenced by the Black Consciousness movement that arose among young black township dwellers in the late 1960s. The South African Students' Organization helped to promote a new sense of racial pride.

While she was in prison, Winnie had learned that Nelson's son by his first marriage, Thembi, had died in an automobile accident; she was saddened that she had been unable to comfort him or share in his sorrow. Nelson not only had lost his son but had been kept wondering for two years about his wife's predicament. His many inquiries went unanswered, and he spent sleepless nights worrying frantically about what had become of her. Years later he wrote to Winnie, "Although I always try to put on a brave face . . . few things disorganize my whole life as much as this particular kind of hardship."

Through all the long years of separation, Nelson and Winnie's love survived. Nelson kept his wife's photo on the shelf next to his bed; every morning, he gently kissed it in remembrance of better days. In April 1976, he wrote to Winnie, "What you perhaps don't know is how I often think and actually picture in mind all that makes you up physically and spiritually — the loving remarks which came daily and the blind eye you've always turned against those numerous irritations that would have frustrated another woman. Sometimes, it's a wonderful experience to think back about precious moments spent with you darling."

By the mid-1970s, Nelson Mandela had been in jail for almost 15 years; none of his writings could be published, yet he clearly remained the most popular leader in South Africa. One supporter observed, "Once you've put a man in prison 'for life,' there's nothing else you can do to him — except kill him, of course. He becomes a power in his own self. The longer Mandela is kept in prison, the more of a focus he becomes for the things we all hope for." Just as Mandela had listened to campfire stories about heroic Zulu warriors when he was a boy, so young African children were being raised on tales of Nelson Mandela, the legendary revolutionary and father of their country.

Nor was the South African regime able to destroy the morale of Mandela and the men on Robben Island, although the intrepid leader once observed that "South Africa's prisons are intended to cripple us so that we should never again have the strength and courage to pursue our ideals." The protests that Mandela led against the prison authorities, combined with international pressures, brought major improvements in prison conditions. Hard labor was

Protests over the government's decree that Afrikaans must be taught in black schools erupted into student riots in Soweto in 1976. Hundreds of rock-throwing youths were shot down in confrontations with police in armored cars.

ended; the men's letters were increased to two a month; the men were allowed to resume their college studies; and a volleyball court was constructed. All Mandela's comrades spoke of his inspirational effect on their lives. "Nelson never gives up," said a fellow prisoner. "He thinks the struggle 24 hours per day in his life."

Winnie Mandela continued her own struggle in the face of enormous government coercion. After her release from prison in 1970, she was given a new banning order that restricted her to the township, placed her under house arrest each night and week-

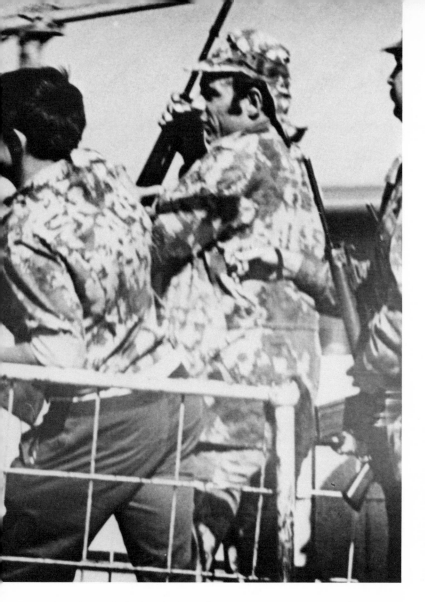

In 1975, the banning orders restricting Winnie Mandela's right to speak in public were lifted. In interviews with journalists, she warned that the South African government's refusal to negotiate with young black militants could only lead to future bloodshed.

end, and forbade her from receiving more than one visitor in her home. She was arrested five times in the 1970s for petty violations of the banning order. Once, a friend stopped by Winnie's house with her nine-month-old baby; the government charged that this represented a security risk. Winnie also survived numerous attacks on her life and property during the 1970s. Bombs were thrown through her windows and her watchdog was poisoned. One night, three men broke into her home and attempted to strangle her but ran off when the loud screams of Winnie's niece woke the neighbors.

The government's crackdown on student unrest shattered hopes that any reform of the apartheid system was imminent. In a letter to Winnie, Mandela wrote how the massacre of black youths felt to him in a sense as though a plant he had nurtured had been torn up by the roots.

In spite of having to endure murder attempts, losing her husband to a life prison sentence, having to send her children out of the country for their education, and being unable to enjoy the close personal relationships with friends that most people take for granted, Winnie, as her friend Helen Joseph said, "emerged from it all as indestructible." The importance of the cause enabled Winnie and Nelson, in their daughter Zindzi's words, to "sacrifice all the material things, to fight for justice, honor and human dignity."

"I have ceased a long time ago to exist as an individual," Winnie said once. "The ideas, the political goals that I stand for, those are the ideas and goals of the people in this country. . . . Whatever they do to me, they do to the people in this country." Surprisingly, when Winnie's bans expired in 1975, the government decided not to impose any new ones. For the first time in 10 years she was able to travel in her country, yet when a reporter asked her if she was enjoying her freedom, she replied, "I am not free. There is no such thing as freedom for me and my people yet."

The truth of Winnie's statement was demonstrated once again in the mid-1970s. In 1976, Prime Minister John Vorster announced his government's plans to expand its apartheid policies in the field of education. What the whites called "Bantu" education (the Afrikaners commonly use the term *Bantu* to refer to the native African population) had always been a cornerstone of the apartheid system; characterized by overcrowded, inferior facilities and high dropout rates, it had always perpetuated African inequality and white supremacy. Dr. Hendrik Verwoerd, a former prime minister and chief advocate of Bantu education, wrote, "There is no place for the Bantu in the European community above the level of certain forms of labor. . . . Natives will be taught from childhood that equality with Europeans is not for them." The Afrikaners now proposed a new regulation that would force African students in the segregated Soweto townships to learn some subjects in the Afrikaner language, Afrikaans, instead of in English. African students formed an organization known as the Soweto Students Representative Council (SSRC) to protest the government's new policy. They did not object to studying the Afrikaans language itself but resented what they believed was another attempt to extend their oppression.

As in so many protests, this particular dispute became a symbol for deep-seated hatred of the system in general; the African students were really condemning the pass laws, the absence of political freedom, the police repression. The protests coincided with a new mood of militancy that swept South Africa in the 1970s. Liberation seemed increasingly possible after 1975, when Angola and Mozambique became independent states through victorious guerrilla wars against white colonial regimes.

Also capturing the imagination of the young students fighting against the Afrikaner regime was a new political organization known as the Black Consciousness movement, founded by university students led by Steve Biko. Black Consciousness activists sought to increase black pride and provide psychological liberation from oppression. As Biko wrote, "Black consciousness is the realization that the black man must rally together with his brothers . . . and operate as a group to rid themselves of the shackles that bind them to perpetual servitude."

On June 16, 1976, the SSRC organized a mass protest against the government's language plan. Twenty thousand African schoolchildren marched through the Soweto townships singing ANC songs and holding banners proclaiming, If we must do Afrikaners, then Vorster must do Zulu! The police released dogs but were unable to stop the children's momentum. As they had done in Sharpeville, the police once again panicked and opened fire on an unarmed crowd, killing a 13-year-old boy and several others; the children threw stones and carried garbage can lids as shields against the police guns. "That is what happens when you want to break these chains of oppression; nothing else seems to matter," wrote Winnie Mandela of the children's brave determination.

The police brutality triggered a yearlong uprising that made Soweto an internationally recognized symbol of the liberation struggle. The Soweto uprising marked an unprecedented scale of revolt: tens of thousands in black ghettos throughout the country participated. The protests quickly became a broad challenge to the entire system of white supremacy. Everything related to apartheid in the townships was attacked. Demonstrators destroyed Bantu government offices and burned down the government-run beer halls and liquor stores. Black youths clashed regularly and fiercely with heavily armed police; protestors barricaded the streets with burning tires, cars, and other debris to prevent police entry into the townships. They boycotted schools, staged massive rallies and marches, and organized a widespread work stoppage. To raise funds and supplies for the protestors and their families, Winnie Mandela helped establish the Black Parents Association.

Police massacres of blacks had punctuated South Africa's history but nothing so terrible had been known: a modern armed force moving against schoolchildren.

—MARY BENSON
South African author

When the uprising spread to other South African cities, the white regime moved decisively to quell it, making mass arrests and stationing army and police units in the townships. The police imposed a reign of terror with tear gas, armored cars, helicopters, roadblock searches, and house-to-house raids, and the death toll of protestors eventually reached 1,000, with more than 4,000 wounded. Thirteen thousand Africans were arrested throughout the country, nearly 5,000 of whom were under the age of 18. Most student leaders were either imprisoned or were forced to flee the country. Steve Biko, the charismatic black leader, was tortured and died while in police detention in September 1977.

"The Soweto uprising," wrote historian James North, "was easily the most profound and widespread upheaval in South African history." The revolt was a profound shock to the white government. Blacks had resolutely stood their ground against the superior firepower of the army and police and had demonstrated their collective refusal to submit to their own oppression. The Soweto uprising was a dramatic radicalizing experience for thousands of protestors; a new generation of activists was born in the crucible of struggle against the apartheid regime.

A demonstrator waves a picture of student leader Steve Biko, who was arrested by police and beaten to death by prison guards in 1977. Continued atrocities against black dissidents led to stronger international criticism of the apartheid regime.

9

Mother of the Country

On May 15, 1977, as the Soweto rebellion began to subside, policemen surrounded Winnie Mandela's home in the early morning hours. She was taken to a Johannesburg police station and informed that she was going to be banished to Brandfort, a poor black town in the isolated, underpopulated Orange Free State, one of the country's four provinces. As the biographer Nancy Harrison recounts, the police commander gloated, "This the end of the road for you, Winnie Mandela. This time we are going to make you pay in a way you will never forget. From now on, you are going to live in Brandfort till you die." The South African government believed that placing Winnie Mandela in exile would finally crush her spirit of resistance; that far removed from the center of political life in the country, she would gradually be forgotten. Little did they know they were sending Winnie Mandela to her greatest triumph.

Winnie had never even heard of the tiny rural village of Brandfort. Her new home was a tiny three-room cement-block house, located in the midst of a barren field of dirt. The house had no electricity, no running water, and no sewer system, and the front

When they send me into exile, it's not me as an individual they are sending. They think with me they can also ban the political ideas . . . I couldn't think of a greater honor.
—WINNIE MANDELA
on being banished
to Brandfort

During the past two decades, Winnie Mandela has emerged as one of the most popular spokespersons for the cause of racial equality. Although physically separated, she and her husband have been united in their roles as the soul of the South African resistance movement.

Winnie Mandela distributes international relief assistance to needy residents of Brandfort, South Africa. In 1977, she was banished to this impoverished village. Displaying her customary strength of purpose, she united the villagers behind a self-improvement program.

and side doors were only openings that could not be closed. Inside, dirt floors were strewn with garbage; behind the house was a pit that served as a toilet. Winnie's furniture could not fit through the narrow doors, so she and Zindzi spent their first night huddled together on a mattress outside in the bitter cold. As Winnie remarked, "Suddenly, our house in Soweto seemed like a palace."

Winnie was outraged by the appalling conditions in the Brandfort ghetto. The Africans there were destitute; their children suffered from malnutrition and had no medical care. Even worse was the hopelessness and habits of deference that blacks had developed after years of oppression. "The police devised this punishment to destroy me morally and spiritually," she said. "They hoped to leave me in complete shreds but seeing the conditions here has made me more determined than I have ever been in my life to show that I will continue ministering to my people and helping them in every way I can."

The blacks in Brandfort had been told by the white authorities that a dangerous Communist was being exiled to their town. The people were warned that anyone who tried to associate with the woman would receive the same fate as her husband, who was imprisoned for life. But most Africans are naturally skeptical of anything the white government says, and people soon began stopping by Winnie's house and greeting her in the street. They also learned to trust Winnie because of her courage and determination in dealing with the white authorities, who strictly enforced segregation in Brandfort.

Winnie of course refused to abide by the restrictions. On her second day in exile, she needed to telephone her attorney in Johannesburg, but the one available public phone was for whites only. Winnie nevertheless waited in line to make her call, ignoring the shouted insults of whites. Finally her turn came and Winnie deliberately prolonged her conversation; when her call was finished, she headed to the grocery store, which also was to be used only by whites, and walked right through the front door. The owner of the store was too stunned by Winnie's brashness to protest, but the other white shoppers fled in horror. Winnie's courage inspired other Africans to follow her lead; soon, blacks could be seen shopping in the white stores and using the telephone. Little black children even began to greet Winnie with the "Amandla" black power salute.

Young South Africans flourish a poster bearing Winnie Mandela's message of support to resistance fighters. Wherever Winnie Mandela appears, crowds of children gather to cheer the "Mother of the Country" and to greet her with the raised fist of the *Amandla* black power salute.

Flanked by her daughters Zindzi (left) and Zeni, Winnie Mandela speaks to reporters after visiting her husband. Although a campaign by international human rights groups to win Mandela's release from prison failed, he and Winnie were permitted to have direct contact in 1984.

Winnie set out to transform her "little Siberia," her place of exile, into a real community. Her friends sent her seeds and seedlings, and soon an oasis of green sprouted in the barren ground. In time her home was surrounded by fruit trees and shrubs, a vegetable garden and flowers, and a lawn that was constantly alive with the joyous sounds of children playing. Winnie's supporters bought medical supplies to help establish a clinic for the township, and she bought a used car to provide a mobile health clinic for Africans who worked on the outlying farms. She also set up a soup kitchen and bakery to help alleviate the malnutrition of the local children.

Blacks in Brandfort gradually began to feel a sense of confidence and community. After spending their entire lives as anonymous victims of apartheid, they derived immense spiritual strength and inspiration from Winnie's courage and heroism. Winnie's close friend Sally Motlana never doubted that she would survive her ordeal in Brandfort. "They will never succeed in building a wall around her," Motlana said. "It doesn't matter where they banish her — homeland, desert, or forest — this woman is so dynamic, she will make the birds sing and the trees rustle wherever she goes."

Winnie became internationally recognized during her exile in the late 1970s and 1980s. Countless diplomats and dignitaries from around the world journeyed to Brandfort to meet the woman Africans now referred to as the "Mother of the Country." Typically, however, Winnie insisted that "I am of no importance as an individual. What I stand for is what they want to banish." Indeed, Winnie seemed more comfortable simply being known as the grandmother of her daughter's children. Her eldest daughter Zeni married Prince Dhlamini of Swaziland, and according to custom, their three children were raised by the maternal grandmother, Winnie, until they reached kindergarten age.

Having her grandchildren with her, along with Zindzi, who stayed in Brandfort during her school breaks, was a great joy and helped make up for all the time Winnie had been separated from her family. The loneliness of exile was a tremendous burden, but Winnie also found it to be a source of great strength. "Each minute," she said, "is a reminder that blackness alone is a commitment in our sick society." When a reporter asked her if she had ever given up hope, Winnie replied, "Of course not. How can I lose hope when I know that in truth this country is ours and that we'll get it back! I know that all this is something I must bear in order to reach that goal."

In April 1982, Winnie received a letter from the Prison Department informing her that Nelson and the other Rivonia defendants had been transferred from Robben Island to Pollsmoor Prison, a maximum-security jail outside Cape Town. At first, Win-

The more conservative Afrikaners remain stubbornly opposed to making even minor concessions to the nonwhite population. Many white South Africans fear that eventually they will be driven from the country if blacks are allowed to gain political power.

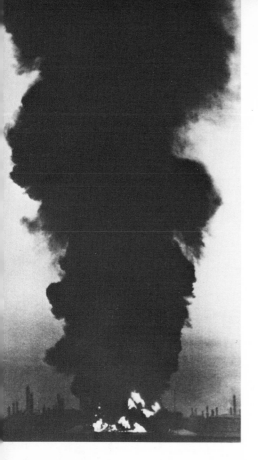

After 15 years of inactivity, Mandela's MK resistance fighters renewed their sabotage strikes against government installations in the early 1980s. The headquarters of the ANC and most other black nationalist groups are now located in other African nations.

nie suspected that because of Nelson's reported ill health, the authorities wanted to bring him closer to better medical facilities. But the real reason, as Mary Benson described, was that Mandela's heroic image had reached almost mythic proportions, even throughout the world. Likewise, his training and education of young political prisoners had become so extensive that Robben Island was commonly referred to as "Mandela University."

At Pollsmoor, Mandela and his companions were housed on the third floor of a prison wing, where despite better food and a greater variety of newspapers and books, conditions were much worse than on Robben Island. Previously, each man had had his own private cell and could move freely about in a friendly communal atmosphere; at Pollsmoor, the six were confined in one large cell in total isolation from the rest of the prison population. Mandela, now 64 years old, was excused from the prison-work detail and spent most of his time reading or tending his small vegetable garden.

On May 12, 1984, Mandela was allowed his first physical contact with Winnie. Most of their marriage together had consisted of glances and brief conversations through a glass partition. On this visit they were able to touch for the first time in more than 20 years. Nelson and Winnie kissed and embraced for a long time; as Winnie said, it was "an experience one just can't put into words."

A short time later, Nelson wrote to Winnie that making his commitment to the freedom struggle would have been much harder had he been able to see clearly the countless hardships that Winnie would be exposed to. In her reply, Winnie admitted that she often felt sad and frustrated that they had been cheated of their best years together. But she clearly had no regrets. "If life is comprised of the things you enumerate and hold dear," Winnie wrote, "I am lost for words due to the fact that in my own small way, life feels a little more monumental, material and demanding of one's innermost soul. That is why the love and warmth that exude from you behind those unkind, concrete, grey, monotonous, and cruel walls simply overwhelms me, especially when I think of those who in the name of the struggle have been deprived of that love."

In 1982, an international campaign to release Mandela was formed to protest the 20th anniversary of his imprisonment. The Security Council of the United Nations called on South Africa to release Mandela and other political prisoners, saying that only then could "meaningful discussion of the future of the country" be achieved. This international support coincided with the political resurgence of the ANC during the early part of the decade, following the near-inactivity of its guerrilla wing, Umkhonto we Sizwe, between 1964, when the Rivonia leadership was captured, and 1976, the time of the Soweto revolt. The exodus of thousands of young militants in the aftermath of the Soweto uprising, however, provided MK with a nucleus of motivated guerrillas. By the early 1980s, MK had developed new infiltration routes and had established a rudimentary organizational presence within the main cities. From 1980 to 1984, ANC guerrillas launched 100 separate attacks against a variety of targets, including heavily fortified police stations, power plants, and oil refineries.

In their most audacious assault, in May 1983, MK exploded a car bomb outside South African Air Force headquarters in Johannesburg; 18 people were killed and 190 wounded. The attack, which also killed several innocent black bystanders, seemed to indicate that the ANC had abandoned its long-standing ban on sparing civilian bystanders in their sabotage campaigns. The white government condemned the ANC for its "terrorist" actions, but most Africans were happy that the MK had finally chosen to attack real instead of merely symbolic targets. From prison, Mandela said he regretted any loss of life caused by the freedom struggle but that it was the white regime's far greater violence that had provoked the Africans' actions. The white government, he said, "must legalize us, treat us like a political party and negotiate with us. Until they do, we will have to live with the armed struggle. It is useless simply to carry on talking. The government has tightened the screws too far."

Nelson Mandela is the power that he is because he is a great man—about that there can be no doubt. Our tragedy is that he has not been around to help douse the flames that are destroying our beautiful country.
—DESMOND M. TUTU
Anglican Bishop of Johannesburg

10

A Time of Destiny

In September 1978, P. W. Botha succeeded John Vorster as head of the National party and prime minister of South Africa. Botha's assumption of power represented a decisive turning point in the political direction of the white minority regime. At a Nationalist party meeting, Botha proclaimed, "We must adapt or we will die." He pledged that his government would design a comprehensive program that would assure white dominance for future generations.

The establishment of radical African governments in Angola, Mozambique, and Zimbabwe, in conjunction with increased ANC guerrilla activity in South Africa, prompted the Botha regime to reformulate its regional policies. From 1980 on, the government has used military aggression combined with economic and political pressure to undermine the stability of its African neighbors to the north. South Africa has provided military and financial support to rebels fighting against the Angola and Mozambique governments. The government has also destroyed the vital infrastructure (railroads,

He can walk with kings and he can walk with beggars. I want to tell P. W. Botha, if he speaks to Nelson Mandela, he speaks to a reasonable man, not a violent man—one of the kindest, most honest, peace-loving men.
—EDDIE DANIELS

Winnie Mandela continues to represent her husband's views on South Africa's racial problems. In 1985, for the first time in 22 years, she was allowed to discuss political matters with him. Since then, she has spoken out in favor of international efforts to isolate her country's apartheid regime.

A black family listens to South African president P. W. Botha announce a new crackdown on opposition groups. Although pressured by strong international criticism, Botha's government has made only minor reforms to date.

port facilities, and pipelines) of countries such as Zambia, Lesotho, Botswana, and Zimbabwe, all of which have provided support to the ANC. Many of these nations have subsequently been compelled to sign nonaggression pacts with the apartheid regime; they have agreed to restrict ANC guerrilla activities within their borders, and in return, South Africa has promised to stop its support for rebel uprisings in those countries. (That promise has rarely been kept.)

While pursuing an aggressive policy abroad, Botha also proposed a series of reforms at home that were calculated to defuse black militancy without losing the advantages of white supremacy. In an attempt to create a black middle class with a stake in the system, the government eased restrictions on black businesses, allowed blacks to obtain long-term leases for their township homes, and permitted black workers to be hired for jobs in skilled occupations.

In order to appease its international critics, the Botha regime also decided to end several petty apartheid restrictions. They removed the blatant Europeans Only signs on public facilities; they scrapped the infamous Immorality and Mixed Marriages acts, which prohibited interracial marriages; and they welcomed black entertainers and sports celebrities to perform in front of racially mixed audiences in Sun City. The government established elected black community councils to handle the day-to-day administration of the townships.

But Botha's reforms were merely cosmetic changes that left the power structure of the white supremacy entirely intact. The homelands, for example, continued to be an integral feature of the regime. From 1961 to 1981, the white government forced more than 3.5 million people to resettle in the homelands; this was one of the largest enforced movements of people in modern world history. By 1980, 10 million of the 23 million Africans in South Africa lived in the homelands. Each "independent" homeland received the appropriate trappings of statehood (a flag, a national anthem, a legislature, a constitution), but they remained utterly dependent on South Africa for their economic and political support. Not a single United Nations country other than South Africa has recognized the political independence of the homelands.

Black Consciousness leader Steve Biko aptly characterized the homelands as "tribal cocoons [that are] nothing else but sophisticated concentration camps." They are massively overcrowded ghettos, resembling Third World refugee camps, located amidst the unspoiled South African countryside. High unemployment, rampant starvation and malnutrition, and appalling health conditions are commonplace. The infant mortality rate for Africans in the homelands is 282 per 1,000 babies, while the figure for whites in South Africa as a whole is 12 per 1,000, the third lowest in the world; barely half of the African children alive at birth survive past the age of 5. South Africa is a wealthy, industrialized country, considerably more advanced than any other African nation, yet the white government has perpetuated itself through oppression.

> *You [Nelson Mandela] are a true leader of our people, we will not rest until you are free. Your release and that of all political prisoners is imperative. Your sacrifice for your people is affirmed. We commit ourselves anew to a free South Africa in which the people shall govern.*
> —The UDF
> in a message intended for Mandela, 1985

The most widely heralded reform of the Botha regime was the 1984 constitutional revision establishing "a new tricameral parliament." The colored (people legally categorized as being of mixed descent) and Indian populations were now represented along with the whites, who still retained a veto over any decisions made by the minority representatives. The new constitution evoked widespread protest across the nation. Africans believed the complete exclusion of the black majority from even token political representation demonstrated once and for all the bankruptcy of the Afrikaner reforms. Eighty percent of the coloreds and Indians boycotted the elections for the new parliament, and more than 400,000 students stayed home from their classes in protest.

Many of the protests against the constitution were spearheaded by the new United Democratic Front (UDF). Founded in August 1983, the UDF was a multiracial alliance of more than 600 antiapartheid organizations, with a combined membership of more than 1 million. The UDF, which mobilized around the slogan "Apartheid Divides, UDF Unites," traced its lineage to the ANC's Congress Alliance; the UDF too was a broad-based popular movement rather than an ideologically oriented political party, and it embraced the principles embodied in the ANC's Freedom Charter. One of its three elected presidents was Albertina Sisulu, wife of Walter Sisulu, who was serving a life sentence with Nelson Mandela. The rise of the UDF marked a crucial turning point in South African politics; it was the first political organization that had been able to harness the militancy that had developed in the African townships after the Soweto uprising.

The inaugural meeting of the tricameral parliament in August 1984 precipitated further demonstrations in the black townships. In October, when the protest spread to Soweto, regular army units were moved into the townships to back up the police. As a regular pattern of violence soon developed in the townships, the police used rubber bullets, tear gas, and birdshot to disperse the crowds of

Africans. Black youths in turn ambushed policemen and government vehicles and barricaded township streets to stop the government troops.

This phase of protests culminated in November with the most successful work stoppage in South Africa in more than 35 years. Eighty percent of the workers in the Transvaal stayed home to demand the withdrawal of the army and police from the townships and the release of all political prisoners. Some 600,000 students joined with the UDF to support the strike in what proved to be the first sustained cooperation between workers and popular organizations in South African history.

In the midst of a deepening political crisis, Prime Minister Botha announced on January 31, 1985, that the South African government was prepared to release Nelson Mandela if he would agree to renounce the use of violence as a legitimate means of achieving political objectives. On February 10, Mandela's daughter Zindzi read her father's stirring reply at a huge rally in Soweto to celebrate the awarding of the 1984 Nobel Peace Prize to anti-apartheid activist Bishop Desmond Tutu. "Let Botha renounce violence. Let him say that he will dismantle apartheid . . . or free all who have been imprisoned, banished or exiled," wrote Mandela. "Too many have died since I went to prison. Too many have suffered for the love of freedom. I cannot sell my birthright nor am I prepared to sell the birthright of the people to be free." Mandela's statement continued, "Only free men can negotiate. . . . Your freedom and mine cannot be separated."

Then, on March 21, 1985, as South African police blocked a funeral procession of 500 people in the Langa township outside the city of Uitenhage, a young boy on a bicycle inadvertently rode ahead and was shot by the police without warning. The police then opened fire indiscriminately and killed 21 marchers. Ironically, the attacks fell on the 25th anniversary of the first Sharpeville/Langa massacre in 1960. In the following days, armored military vehicles mounted roadblocks at every intersection, and heavily armed soldiers patrolled the streets. The

Children wait in line for food in a drought-stricken area of South Africa. Malnutrition, disease, poverty, and unemployment are rife in the black homeland areas, which receive little financial assistance from the South African government.

Zindzi Mandela reads a statement by her father refusing the conditional terms for his release from prison. In 1985, the government offered to free him in exchange for his agreement to renounce the use of armed resistance to apartheid.

scene in Langa and other eastern Cape townships soon resembled a war zone: the streets were blackened by bombs and barricades, and government buildings and properties owned by whites were torched.

After "Bloody Thursday" at Langa, South African police shifted their tactics, employing heavier weaponry and implementing shoot-to-kill orders against the protestors. Botha boasted on ABC television's *Nightline* program, "I am going to keep order in South Africa and nobody is going to stop me." Yet it was evident that the Africans' mass defiance since August 1984 had escalated into a broad radical challenge to the foundations of white power. The townships were ungovernable; local apartheid institutions such as black community councils and Bantu schools completely collapsed. Funerals and memorial services were scenes of open defiance, where demonstrators unfurled the banners of the outlawed ANC and South African Communist party and speakers called for an immediate end to white rule. Winnie Mandela defied the government's bans and returned from Brandfort to Soweto to speak at a funeral for victims of police shootings. She proclaimed, "This is our country. In the same way as you have had to bury our children today, so shall the blood of these heroes we buried today be avenged."

By July 1985, it appeared that the white government had lost control over most of the black townships in the eastern Cape and Transvaal, and the entire nation seemed to be on the brink of civil war. More than 500 people had been killed in the protests since the previous August. On July 20, Botha declared a nationwide state of emergency, the first since the emergency imposed in the wake of the Sharpeville massacre. The police were given unlimited power to search homes without warrants and detain protestors indefinitely without trial. More army units were deployed throughout the black townships, and massive use of firepower became the government's only way to put down the disturbances.

The huge protests suddenly brought the horrors of apartheid to the attention of the American public. Night after night, television broadcasts presented graphic images of young African boys battling tanks with sticks and stones while South African police savagely beat and whipped black protestors. In the United States, outraged protestors urged all American businesses to cease operations in South Africa and called upon universities, cities, and pension funds to divest their stock in companies that refused to do so. More and more people have come to believe that those individuals who continue to own stock in companies that do business in South Africa are indirectly participating in the repression.

The coffin of a Soweto student slain by the police is carried by her friends. In 1985 the government imposed restrictions on large funeral processions after they became the focus of black fury against repeated incidents of police brutality.

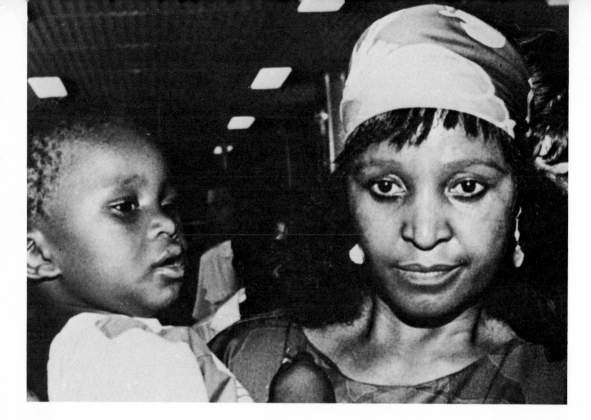

Winnie Mandela holds her grandson Zondwa as she attempts to return to her home in Soweto, from which she was banned. Clashes between police and black demonstrators exploded into a series of bloody riots in the townships in 1985.

The divestment campaign sparked the largest wave of student protests in the United States since the Vietnam War and rekindled memories of the 1960s. Students at Yale University, in Connecticut, set up a mock shantytown in the middle of a campus quadrangle, calling it "Winnie Mandela City." Students at Rutgers University, in New Jersey, held a three-week sit-in in their student center (which they renamed Nelson Mandela Center) to pressure the university administration to divest its stock portfolio. Other sectors of American society protested against the apartheid regime as well. Numerous states and cities passed strong divestment legislation, and the United States Congress overwhelmingly passed limited sanctions against South Africa. In the fall of 1985, several major banks announced they would no longer lend money to the South African government or to businesses there.

The upsurge in the international protests coincided with an important new development within South Africa. On November 30, 1985, 33 African trade unions joined together to form the Congress of South Africa Trade Unions (COSATU), the largest organization of black workers in South African history, with a total membership of more than 500,000. Black workers now had the strategic power to mount a large-scale withdrawal of labor from the modern South African economy, which was increasingly dependent on their skills. COSATU forged important links with the United Democratic Front, and at its July 1987 conference it openly endorsed the ANC's Freedom Charter as its own political platform. The National Union of Mineworkers, the most important union within COSATU, even elected Nelson Mandela as its honorary life president in 1986. On May 1, 1986, 1.5 million workers responded to COSATU's call for a nationwide stayaway to support demands for increased wages and political freedoms.

Signs at Columbia University in New York call for divestment of school funds from companies that have business ties to South Africa. Mandela has repeatedly asked that all nations impose tough economic sanctions on South Africa until it ends its apartheid policies.

In September 1986, 177 black miners were killed in an accident at Kinross. COSATU leaders blamed the deaths on the hazardous conditions in the mines and organized a huge protest rally. As speakers were exhorting the workers to support new strikes, a great cry of "Viva Winnie Mandela" echoed throughout the stadium and Winnie Mandela dramatically approached the microphone. "We accept that the time for talking has come to an end," she declared. "The moment you stop digging Pretoria's gold and diamonds, we will be free." Winnie proclaimed that "there will be a day soon when we say 'this is the last day; we are taking over.'"

The 1984–86 uprisings dramatically confirmed the depths of black dissatisfaction with the white government, but Winnie's optimistic prediction still has not come to pass. The ANC has offered to negotiate with the Afrikaner regime for a peaceful transition to a black majority government, but it has insisted that negotiations could take place only if Mandela and other prisoners are released and the

Riot police with tear gas guns stand guard over a demonstration by black trade unionists. Unable to suppress black unrest, the government has granted a few black labor organizations the right to represent the country's millions of exploited black workers.

apartheid institutions dismantled. The essence of the problem continues to be the fact that democratic equality for the Africans would inevitably lead to a loss of power for the whites, and the ruling Afrikaners remain adamant about preserving their privileges.

Still, hopeful signs of change do exist. Sections of the white community have now accepted the idea that a lasting settlement will only be possible with ANC participation. On July 13, 1987, a delegation of 60 white apartheid opponents made up of writers, politicians, clergy, and business people met with ANC leaders in Dakar, Senegal, in western Africa. Both sides endorsed the goal of a nonracial democracy in South Africa, and the white dissidents proclaimed that only the unconditional release of Nelson Mandela and other political prisoners could lead to any meaningful change in South Africa. Thus, even after 25 years in prison, Nelson Mandela still remains the focus for the hopes and aspirations of Africans. At the age of 70, Nelson Mandela dreams of one day joining his wife Winnie on their long-awaited walk to freedom.

Mandela's defiance of apartheid continues to inspire the South African resistance movement. As he declared in 1961, "The struggle is my life. I will continue fighting for freedom until the end of my days."

Further Reading

Attwell, Michael. *South Africa, Background to the Crisis.* London: Sidgwick & Jackson, 1986.

Benson, Mary. *Nelson Mandela: The Man and the Movement.* New York: Norton, 1986.

Biko, Steve. *I Write What I Like.* Edited by Aelred Stubbs, C.R. London: Boerdean Press, 1978.

First, Ruth. *117 Days.* London: Penguin, 1982.

Gerhart, Gail. *Black Power in South Africa.* Berkeley: University of California Press, 1978.

Goodwin, June. *Cry Amandla!* New York: Africana Press, 1984.

Harrison, David. *The White Tribe of Africa.* Berkeley: University of California Press, 1981.

Harrison, Nancy. *Winnie Mandela: Mother of a Nation.* London: Victor Gollancz, 1985.

Haskins, Jim. *Winnie Mandela: Life of Struggle.* New York: Putnam, 1988.

Hoobler, Dorothy, and Thomas Hoobler. *Nelson and Winnie Mandela.* New York: Franklin Watts, 1987.

Kane-Berman, John. *Soweto: Black Revolt, White Reaction.* Johannesburg, South Africa: Ravan, 1983.

Lawson, Don. *South Africa.* New York: Franklin Watts, 1986.

Lelyveld, Joseph. *Move Your Shadow.* London: Mowbray, 1982.

Lodge, Tom. *Black Politics in South Africa Since 1945.* Johannesburg, South Africa: Ravan, 1983.

Lutuli, Albert. *Let My People Go.* New York: Collins, 1962.

Mandela, Nelson. *The Struggle Is My Life.* New York; Pathfinder, 1986.

Mandela, Winnie. *Part of My Soul Went with Him.* New York: Norton, 1984.

Mandela, Zindzi, and Peter Mugubane. *Black As I Am.* Los Angeles: Guild of Tutors Press of International College, 1978.

Osmond, Roger. *The Apartheid Handbook.* New York: Penguin, 1975.

Troup, Freda. *South Africa: An Historical Introduction.* New York: Penguin, 1975.

Tutu, Desmond. *Crying in the Wilderness.* London: Mowbray, 1982.

Chronology

July 18, 1918	Nelson Mandela born near Umtata, South Africa
Sept. 26, 1934	Winnie Madikizela born in Pondoland, South Africa
1941	Nelson Mandela studies law in Johannesburg
1943	Forms Youth League of the African National Congress with Oliver Tambo and Walter Sisulu
March 1944	Elected general secretary of the African National Congress
1950	Becomes president of Youth League
1952	Coordinates Defiance Campaign
1955	African National Congress Freedom Charter promulgated
Dec. 2, 1956	Nelson Mandela and 156 others arrested for treason
June 14, 1958	Marries Winnie Madikizela
March 21, 1960	Sharpeville massacre
March 1961	Nelson Mandela acquitted of treason
April 1961	Goes underground and forms Umkhonto we Sizwe (MK)
Jan. 1962	Tours Africa and England
Aug. 5, 1962	Arrested by South African police
June 11, 1964	Sentenced to life imprisonment on Robben Island
May 12, 1969	Winnie Mandela arrested and imprisoned for 17 months
June 16, 1976	Soweto uprising begins
Aug. 1976	Winnie Mandela imprisoned
Dec. 23, 1976	Banished to Brandfort
April 1982	Nelson Mandela transferred to Pollsmoor Prison
May 1984	Nelson and Winnie Mandela have first contact visit in more than 20 years
1984–1986	Mass revolts against apartheid occur throughout South Africa
Feb. 10, 1985	Nelson Mandela rejects conditional release offered by President Botha
1987	African National Congress and white apartheid opponents sign joint manifesto calling for Nelson Mandela's release

Index

John Vail is an instructor in political science at Rutgers University, where he is currently a Ph.D. candidate. A graduate of the University of Chicago, he is also the author of *David Ben-Gurion* and *Fidel Castro* in the Chelsea House series WORLD LEADERS—PAST & PRESENT.

Arthur M. Schlesinger, jr., taught history at Harvard for many years and is currently Albert Schweitzer Professor of the Humanities at City University of New York. He is the author of numerous highly praised works in American history and has twice been awarded the Pulitzer Prize. He served in the White House as special assistant to Presidents Kennedy and Johnson.

PICTURE CREDITS

AP/Wide World Photos: pp. 15, 20, 54, 60, 66, 69, 74, 80, 90, 94, 102, 104; Bettmann Archive: pp. 16, 17, 18, 24, 25, 27; International Defence & Aid Fund for Southern Africa: pp. 2, 12, 22, 26, 28, 32, 34, 36, 38, 39, 40, 42, 43, 44, 46, 49, 50, 56, 59, 62, 63, 64, 70, 77, 78, 82, 83; Reuters/Bettmann Newsphotos: pp. 37, 53, 65, 81, 87, 105; Donna Sinisgalli: p. 19; United Nations: pp. 14, 21, 29, 35, 76; UPI/Bettmann Newsphotos: pp. 37, 53, 65, 81, 87

MACFARLAND JR.
SCHOOL LIBRARY
BORDENTOWN, N.J.